Behold the Lilies

Behold the Lilies

JESUS AND THE CONTEMPLATION OF NATURE—A PRIMER

H. Paul Santmire

CASCADE *Books* · Eugene, Oregon

BEHOLD THE LILIES
Jesus and the Contemplation of Nature—A Primer

Cascade Books
An Imprint of Wipf and Stock Publishers
199 W. 8th Ave., Suite 3
Eugene, OR 97401

www.wipfandstock.com

PAPERBACK ISBN: 978-1-5326-1647-1
HARDCOVER ISBN: 978-1-4982-4028-4
EBOOK ISBN: 978-1-4982-4027-7

Cataloging-in-Publication data:

Names: Santmire, H. Paul.

Title: Behold the lilies : Jesus and the contemplation of nature—a primer / H. Paul Santmire.

Description: Eugene, OR: Cascade Books, 2017 | Includes bibliographical references.

Identifiers: ISBN: 978-1-5326-1647-1 (PAPERBACK) | ISBN: 978-1-4982-4028-4 (HARD-COVER) | ISBN: 978-1-4982-4027-7 (EBOOK).

Subjects: LCSH: Nature—Religious aspects—Christianity | Ecotheology | Human ecology—Religious aspects.

Classification: BT695.5 S32 2017 (print) | BT695.5 (ebook).

Manufactured in the U.S.A.

To Gary

"Behold the lilies of the field, how they grow: they neither toil nor spin, yet I tell you even Solomon in all his glory was not arrayed like one of these."

—MATTHEW 6:28-29 (AUTHOR'S TRANSLATION)

Contents

CONTENTS

Introduction

WHY THIS PRIMER?

Contemplate nature? As a follower of Jesus? Yes. That's what I believe Jesus commands his disciples to do when he says, "Behold the lilies" (Matt 6:28, author's translation). But this is a neglected, if not totally ignored, theme in contemporary Christian theology. Let me explain.

In these times of global crisis, few Christians dispute the need for people of faith to address ecological and related issues of justice and sustainability. Under the rubric of ecology, the world of nature has now become a major theological concern for virtually all Christian churches. Evangelical, mainline Protestant, Roman Catholic, and Orthodox leaders have been speaking and writing about ecological issues vociferously in recent years. The global literature on the Christian faith and ecology is now huge. Pope Francis' widely acclaimed 2015 encyclical, *Laudato Si': On Care for Our Common Home*, is perhaps the most prominent example of these ecumenical trends.[1]

I myself have participated in such discussions for more than forty years, both "on the stump" and in the form of five books on ecological theology, beginning in 1970 with my programmatic study, *Brother Earth: Nature, God, and Ecology in a Time of Crisis* and culminating in 2014—so I then thought—with my spiritual testament, *Before Nature: A Christian Spirituality*.[2] I am well aware that, today, new publications on Christianity and ecology number in the hundreds every few years, a growth trend that shows no signs of abating. Why then this primer?

I could offer this rationale: *let a thousand flowers bloom!* That popular saying attributed to Mao Zedong *does* make some sense in our context, given the urgencies of our planetary ecojustice crisis. Why not one more publication in this field!? Do everything you can! Who knows whose hearts might be touched?! But my purpose here is much more personal.

It pertains to Jesus, as I indicated at the outset. *I have written this primer because Jesus told me to do so and my desire is to obey him.* For me, this is a fresh hearing of Jesus' voice. I have often pondered Jesus' words about the lilies, but I have never heard them before—*as a command.* Nor, as far as I am aware, has any other modern theological or spiritual writer heard them in precisely this way.

This is the spiritual logic that I now find compelling. According to Jesus' last testament at the end of the Gospel of Matthew, his followers are called to teach all people to obey everything he has commanded (Matt 28:19–20). And one of Jesus' commands, not often recognized as such, is precisely this: "Behold the lilies . . ." I will explain presently why I prefer the word "Behold," rather than the more familiar translation, "Consider." This is my point here. Jesus, I believe, has commanded his followers, me among them, to behold the lilies—or, read more generally, to contemplate nature.

But how are we who consider ourselves to be followers of Jesus to understand his command? And once we have done our best to figure that out for ourselves, how should we teach his command to others? *Behold the Lilies* is one idiosyncratic response to these two questions. That is *the occasion* of this little book.

Now regarding this book's *scope.* It *is* a primer, intended for adult readers of any age or station in life, especially those who are claimed by the cares of this world, to whom Jesus spoke when he celebrated the lilies of the field (see Matt 6:25). You are concerned with many things. *You are busy.* I get it. I know that numerous serious souls in these times often prefer discussions of issues important to them that are brief and to the point. But how to do that in this case?

Of course, as any good teacher knows, to communicate meaningfully with anyone, writers or speakers have to understand the language and the culture of the world in which they're trying to teach. Brevity's important, to be sure, but speaking a language that's accessible to today's generations is all the more important. To communicate, authors must understand the questions being raised—and the questions not being raised—in our increasingly post-religious world in North America.

I'm taking it for granted here, as I've already indicated, that the world in which we live *is* a world in crisis in many ways, above all a world driven by legitimate fears about the ecological future of planet Earth, our common home, as Pope Francis has taught us to say. Nature, as we know it in ordinary experience, is profoundly at risk and, with nature, humankind itself, especially the poor of the Earth. I believe that many, religious, non-religious, or otherwise spiritually engaged, are deeply concerned about these issues. I also believe that followers of Jesus, among whom I number myself, must continue to address these issues forthrightly and thoroughly from the perspective of their faith—among these issues what it means to contemplate nature. At the same time, I also am aware that numerous serious souls in these times may not be ready to explore, perhaps not even willing to hear, yet another traditional theological approach to such matters.

I therefore have chosen what might be called, if you will permit this exuberant expression, a *circumambulatory pedagogy*. This means coming at the teaching challenge from many directions, by walking around it, as it were: speaking more suggestively than didactically. The Christian spiritual master of the nineteenth century, Søren Kierkegaard, called this kind of teaching method indirect communication. Jesus himself remains the unsurpassed example of this kind of pedagogy, especially insofar as he taught in parables.

In a word, you approach the teaching challenge not by pursuing some kind of logical argument that unfolds sequentially over the course of many chapters, but *episodically*, with the hope that this will allow your hearers—or your readers—to "get it" that way. You tell them stories or you reflect about experiences of your own or you raise questions that they might not have thought about. You offer them a variety of handles to reach for, which they can take hold of in any order, whenever they have time to do so. And you make it possible for them, in the midst of their sometimes compulsively busy world, to grasp one handle at a time, with some sense of accomplishment.

Contrast the approach that I took in my most recent—and *much* longer—book, *Before Nature*, to which I have already referred. There I warned readers in my Preface that *Before Nature* was *not* the kind of book they could read cover-to-cover during their next flight to London. In contrast, this primer, *Behold the Lilies,* will easily fit into your backpack, next to your iPad, either the book itself or on your Kindle, as you board your flight. Dip into this book here and there at 35,000 feet. Perhaps even try to read *all of it* (!!!), should you discover that you can't sleep at all.

Likewise for any spiritual pilgrim or any inquiring soul who has many cares on his or her mind, but who still is searching for some kind of faith

3

that makes sense in these uncertain and perilous times of ecological and political crisis: this primer is designed to rest on the night table next to your bed for easy access, should you choose to keep it there for a spell and visit it, now and again, as I hope you will. Read, and let these reflections simmer internally, one by one, but not necessarily all at once. Discover new insights, if you're so inspired. But don't feel rushed to finish this book right away. Let the Spirit move you at your own pace.

To the same end, I won't ask you to deal with lengthy footnotes or with any kind of scholarly bibliography here, this in order to facilitate your dipping into this book on that flight to London or just before you retire at night. I will tuck any legally necessary references far away at the back of the book.

On the other hand, I do hope to challenge the readers of this primer personally, in order to make this reading experience worth your while as you ponder how you might respond to Jesus and, in particular, to his command to behold the lilies. I also hope that some readers will get hooked enough on what follows to want to consult the annotated "For Further Reading" section at the end. My intention is that these references will give you an idea of how rich and diverse Christian reflections about nature and ecology and ecojustice have become in our era. This little book will help you the most, I believe, when read in the context of that broader ecumenical discussion.

My goal in *Behold the Lilies*, in sum, is just this, no more, no less, but nevertheless critically important in my view: *to entice you to contemplate nature, as I believe Jesus would have us do.* Or I should be more direct. My goal here is *to convince you that if you want to be a follower of Jesus you must contemplate nature.* It's not as if you can contemplate nature whenever you feel like doing so, say, when you're on vacation in the White Mountains of New Hampshire. On the contrary, the contemplation I have in mind belongs to the heart of your discipleship every day, along the streets of Chicago, if that's where you live. Behold the oak tree at the corner of your street. Behold the—now increasingly rare—sight of the monarch butterfly on a milkweed that's growing in an abandoned lot next door. Contemplate nature. It's not optional. It's a command.

But before I explore that command, I want to consider its object, "the lilies," lest there be any confusion about the matter. It may come as a surprise to those who have cherished this text, but we don't really know which flowers Jesus had in mind, when he issued the command. "Lilies" is the traditional translation. But that doesn't tell us all that much. Typical American church-goers might immediately think of Easter lilies. But that won't work, at least not botanically. In Israel today, avid explorers sometimes can find a kind of white lily distantly related to our Easter lilies. But to do that, you have to head high up into the mountains. Such flowers aren't found in "the fields." Even biblical scholars with botanical interests haven't been able to identify the flowers to which Jesus was referring with any certainty. We should probably therefore think of some lovely wild flowers, which grew in fields and which most people in first-century Palestine would have immediately recognized. On the other hand, until someone comes up with a better explanation about the particular flowers Jesus had in mind, the traditional translation, "lilies of the field," seems to be perfectly acceptable, as long as we don't make too much of it.

Now concerning the word *behold* itself. I use it deliberately, as you will already have noticed. Much depends, of course, on how we translate Jesus' words, as we have them in the Greek New Testament. "*Consider* the lilies" is the familiar rendering of this text. But that word doesn't convey the intensity of Jesus' speech. While the Greek word itself doesn't tell us all that much, since it wasn't widely used in the first century (not surprisingly, it only appears *once* in the entire New Testament), it does offer us some fascinating nuances. In common usage, it appears to have meant "examine closely," "scrutinize," even "rivet your attention."

This suggests that you are to *focus on the flowers themselves*. You are *not* being called upon to do some kind of prudential calculation *in your own mind*, which is what the word "consider" tends to suggest. You're not being asked to figure out how *you* can be more dependent upon God, for example. Rather, you're being called upon to contemplate *the beautiful flowers* right in front of you—whatever the species of flower might be. Hence the translation "behold."

If there's any doubt about the matter, that should be quickly dispelled once we recall Jesus' enthusiastic announcement after he talks about the beautiful flowers he has in mind: "for even Solomon, in all his glory, was not arrayed like one of these" (Matt 6:29). This is Jesus' meaning, clearly: those are *glorious* flowers! Those flowers are *amazing*! Those flowers are *gorgeous*! So *behold* them!

That the Sermon on the Mount, where this discourse about the lilies of the field is to be found, continues by referring to God's care for *humans*, announcing that God provides clothing for us, as God provides lilies as

5

a kind of beautiful covering for the grass of the field, (Matt 6:30) by no means undercuts Jesus' celebration of those glorious flowers *in themselves*. Whatever we humans may learn about our own lives from contemplating the lilies of the field, in other words, the premise of Jesus' discourse is that those flowers are more beautiful than Solomon in all his glory, and that we should therefore behold them.

I learned this translation many years ago from that great twentieth-century Lutheran theologian of nature, Joseph Sittler. This is his eloquent reading of Matthew 6:28: "[O]ne is precisely *not* saying, 'Look at those lilies.' The word 'behold' lies upon that which is beheld with a kind of tenderness which suggests that things in themselves have their own wondrous authenticity and integrity. I am called upon in such a saying not simply to 'look' at a non-self but to 'regard' things with a kind of spiritual honoring of the immaculate integrity of things which are not myself."[3]

As far as I know, Sittler came upon this reading of the lilies text on his own. But doubtless many other writers and poets and painters have celebrated that kind of contemplation of such flowers, in many cultural settings. Søren Kierkegaard was one of these. Commenting on Jesus' words, he said of the lily: "See how it stands in loveliness at your feet; do not despise it; indeed it still waits for you that you may enjoy its beauty! See how it sways back and forth, shakes everything from it so that it may continue to be lovely! See how it sports with the wind, quivers with every movement, so that quiet again it may rejoices in its happy existence! See how gentle it is, always willing to jest and play, while by yielding it still triumphs over the most violent storm!"[4]

This book presupposes such experiences. In one way or another, the compact reflections that follow all have this in common. They explore a variety of ways to follow Jesus' command to *behold the lilies*—and, by what I take to be a clear implication, to *behold nature more generally or to contemplate nature*. This implies, further, as Sittler's language attests—and as Kierkegaard's discourse also suggests—that in what follows we will be angling to recognize and then to celebrate *the integrity of nature, apart from human-centered values*; and thereafter, as we recall Jesus' command, to discern how we might teach others how to contemplate nature as Jesus would have us do.

These reflections have some other things in common, too, although this won't always be obvious. The teacher who announced "Behold the lilies" so forthrightly, was obviously not just interested in flowers. This was the same teacher who also declared, in his inaugural address, as we have it early on in the Gospel of Luke: "The Spirit of the Lord is upon me, because he has anointed me to bring good news to the poor. He has sent me to proclaim release to the captives and recovery of sight to the blind, to let the oppressed go free" (Luke 4:18). As a matter of course, therefore, as I explore what it means to contemplate nature in the reflections that follow, I will also take notice of the needs of the poor and the oppressed creatures of this world, all of whom groan in travail (see Rom 8:22). For Jesus, beholding the creatures of nature and responding to the cries of the poor go hand-in-hand, a motif that attentive readers will see emerging in these reflections again and again.

Further, as Jesus' declaration in his inaugural address—"The Spirit of the Lord is *upon me*"—suggests, Jesus' teaching typically is *self-referential*, implicitly if not explicitly. On the one hand, Jesus frequently taught in a commanding voice, as his repeated utterances in the Sermon on the Mount illustrate: "You have heart that it was said . . . , but I say to you . . ." (e.g., Matt 5:27–28). In this book I'm highlighting his command to "Behold the lilies," which is no less an imperative, I believe, than others, such as "Follow me" (e.g., Matt 4:19).

On the other hand, Jesus' commands can only rightly be understood in light of the One who speaks them, as many in his own time apparently recognized, when they questioned his authority (e.g. Matt 21:23). Who is he? What is his mission? What is his destiny? Accordingly, at points along the way, I will invite readers to think about the One who speaks the command to behold the lilies, about his life, his death, his resurrection, and the cosmic scope of his ministry.

I will accent this focus on Jesus, too, by stationing a biblical text that pertains to him at the beginning of each chapter. All these scriptural references will recall a life-moment in the story of Jesus or a Gospel explication of that story's meaning. Each is intended to tie the immediately ensuing reflections in some manner to Jesus himself. While, then, in what follows I will be ranging far and wide to explore some of the dynamics of contemplating nature as I have experienced them and thought about them for many years, I will always have the concrete command of Jesus to behold the lilies in mind and, with that, Jesus himself, as we know him in the Gospel traditions.

More generally, it will be apparent throughout that I'm fascinated with Jesus. I hope that the texts at the beginning of each set of reflections will remind the reader of this existential fact. Indeed, for me it's more than a fascination. For me, Jesus is the luminescent spiritual center of this primer, even though his life and his teaching are not explicitly at the forefront of many of the encounters and explorations narrated in this book. His command to behold the lilies is the spiritual premise of everything else, even when there's no mention of his name or his teachings in any particular discussion.

Two last prefatory comments now, before I turn you loose to read one of the selections that follow. First: I have arranged these reflections under two headings, *Encounters* and *Explorations*. The Encounters focus on immediate contemplative relationships of my own with nature or on behalf of nature, as a follower of Jesus. The Explorations presuppose such relationships, but are more ruminant. In the latter group, I try to understand, in some modest measure, what's happening when I encounter nature contemplatively as a follower of Jesus. Still, as I say, all of these reflections stand on their own and all can be read in any order.

Second: My theme of beholding the lilies is also hidden in this book's dedication. *Behold the Lilies* is affectionately dedicated to my brother, the Rev. Gary C. Santmire, who has been cultivating and contemplating glorious flowers—including lilies—much of his adult life and sharing many of them with others, among them myself. His has been a holy vocation of love and beauty for which I am deeply grateful.

H. P. S.

Watertown, Massachusetts

Easter 2017

PART 1

Encounters

1

Scything with God

"He said to them, 'Come away to a deserted place
all by yourselves and rest for a while.'"

(MARK 6:31)

My family owns an old farmhouse at Hunt's Corner, in rural, southwestern Maine, in the foothills of New Hampshire's White Mountains. For me, this is a place of spiritual knowing—a deserted place, in a biblical sense—where I can contemplate nature in peace. When I get away to Hunt's Corner, to a familiar place that almost always surprises me, I often behold a world of amazing beauty and striking diversity of plants and animals and contours of the land and of the clouds, particularly when I scythe.

Thankfully, I've never had to decide whether or not to scythe the field of daylilies south of our house. That land belongs to the postcard picturesque, little white New England church next door, which was moved up from the valley to that place, we've been told, in the second half of the nineteenth century. Call this a holy place, the daylily field included. That's why I wouldn't want to scythe that field, even if I could. For me, it's sacrosanct.

The common orange daylilies there have gone wild and spread widely over the years. Members of that church don't cultivate that field. Instead, those several hundreds of bright orange flowers seem to take care of themselves. They apparently don't allow other plants to take root in their midst. And their beauty's deceptively ordinary, so much so that it wasn't until many years after we had begun to cultivate our own land that I happened one day to stop in my tracks to contemplate them. My God, I thought to myself, I'm beholding the daylilies of that field! How long had it taken me to discover the obvious: that Solomon in all his glory was not arrayed like one of these!?

But it's my scything with the God, in whose name that church had been built and then relocated, which I want to describe here, even though when I think about it, I realize that that the daylilies of that field define everything else I want to say.

I love to scythe the field to the north that separates our plain nineteenth-century house from the wooded slopes beyond and above. I scythe that swath of variously sized and elegantly configured ferns and purple asters and goldenrod and yarrow and meadow rue and daisies and black-eyed susans and evening primroses and the differentiated patches of stunning grasses and the innumerable seedlings of white pine, hemlock, ash, maple, birch, and meadowsweet every fall, and I do so with a passion.

Why this passion? The exercise itself, to begin with, is good. I work hard to take care of this tired old body. There is something, too, about scything that focuses the mind and quiets the heart, notwithstanding all the physical effort required. In fields that have not been tilled for many years, such as ours, the scyther must carefully attend to the sometimes bulging contours of the land, so as not to jam the carefully sharpened blade into the coarse, rocky soil. As one attains a rhythm with the swinging scythe, one must see through the jungle of plants in front of one's feet and adjust the course of the scythe in flight, so as to be able to cut the plants as closely as possible to the earth and yet to avoid that jarring experience, that dull thud, that clanking, which results from faulty swings when the blade jams into the soil. When the swing is right, however, and the blade is sharp, the cutting feels effortless. In my experience, the scyther is then attuned to the rhythm of the field. Such moments almost always leave me contented. But there are other benefits of scything, too.

Scything keeps our back field from turning into part of the forest, as it would quickly do without that kind of yearly attention. I do not mean to demean the forest, by any means. The trees on those slopes north of our house have their own awesome standing, without a doubt, especially the colossal, hundred-year old white pines. But the field has its particular kind of mean-ing, too, which I want to help preserve. Hence my scything. Without that work, the forest would overtake the field in no time. Ash trees, for example. During the first few weeks of the spring following my fall scything, hun-dreds of ash seedlings soon sprout up to a height of maybe ten inches. They are already tiny trees by the time the next fall rolls around. So, if you want to have a field, as I do, you must care for it, lest the forest take over.

The field as I see it—a thought that reflects the perspective of some New England transcendentalists—mediates between our house, on the one hand, with its variegated gardens and its modest lawns, and the forest beyond, on the other hand, where one can catch signs of the bears, the moose, the porcupines, the foxes, and the other creatures of the wild that sometimes edge their ways toward our house; or one can contemplate the red-tailed hawks and the crows, the swallows and the goldfinches, the hum-mingbirds and the doves, the grouse and the wild turkeys, and the occa-sional purple grosbeak or downy woodpecker or woodcock that soar above or fly nearby or otherwise announce their presence from time to time. The whole area where I scythe is a rich meeting place for many creatures. So I scythe that back field once a year in contentment, not just for the exercise, but also for the sake of reaffirming its right to be and its larger meanings.

Scything, I should also point out, brings with it more than the good exercise and preservation of the beautiful spaces between our house and the woods. The scyther, in our part of the world, must contend with the blackflies or the mosquitoes or the ticks, messengers of pain in their own ways, depending on the season or the rainfall. Once, more ominously, my scythe dislodged a nest of bald-faced hornets, tucked at the base of some high, thick grass. When I instantly realized what I had done, it was too late. They were upon me in droves.

That experience then impelled me to run faster than I think I had ever run, at least since the days when I played soccer in high school. I ran as urgently as I did, not only so that I could avoid the onslaught of the hornet stings, which already were painful enough, but also to save my life. Many years before, when I was in my thirties, I had been stung on my leg by three such creatures along a New Hampshire mountain trail and had had to limp back to my car and drive to an emergency room, twenty miles away, in shock. I could have died, due to what was revealed to me then for the first time to be a severe allergy to insect stings. In this respect, never mind the good exercise and the integrity of the field, scything also keeps me honest about the world of nature. All the wonderful creatures of God's good earth are not always our friends. Only people who never leave their homes or their automobiles or their offices can believe such a fantasy.

This brings me to a still darker truth that I sometimes ponder while I am scything, with particular reference to *our* field. We sometimes refer to this field as "the pipeline." For me, that bland expression isn't bland at all. It has an impact on my consciousness like the thunder and the lightning that occasionally roll over our house and our gardens and the field and on into the woods beyond and above. Our field covers, in very small measure, a pipeline which day and night delivers oil hundreds of miles from Portland, Maine to Montreal, Canada. Sometimes helicopters from the pipeline company shatter the silence of the field, as they roar by at low altitudes and high speeds, inspecting that pipeline. It can be frightening. So, on any given day as I scythe, I think of that fateful black gold pulsing through the pipe buried beneath my feet. And I realize how deeply my own world in rural Maine is bound up with the dynamics of globalized industrial society everywhere, with the threats and the realities of warfare in the Middle East, in particular, and with global warming, more generally. Even more sobering is this ominous fact: before too long, toxic tar-sands oil from Canada might be flowing through that pipeline, moving, in this case, from Montreal to Portland.

This image then sometimes hovers over my mind, especially in the aftermath of one of those helicopter fly-overs: the grim reaper of Death of course carries a scythe! Forces are at work around the globe in these times that threaten the sustainability of human life on this planet and the future of many other creatures as well. Don't those forces—first-century Christians thought of them as the "principalities and powers" of Death—dwarf in significance anything that transpires in one minuscule life like mine, hidden away at times out in the field and surrounded by what some think of as nature's "pristine beauty"? What is my contemplation of nature when I am scything, however good and beautiful it might be in my own eyes, compared to that global scything by those principalities and powers?

Still, I typically scythe in peace. How this is humanly possible in these times of global crisis and cosmic alienation is a question with which I have been wrestling since my first book, *Brother Earth*, more than forty years ago. Notwithstanding all the ambiguities, however, I hope to continue to scythe with such inner serenity as long as I have the physical strength that this traditional practice requires, because when I scythe, in addition to everything else, beyond the good and the beautiful and the ominous and the portentous, I am not only engaged with *God* at that moment, but blessedly engaged.

As I look down the sloping field as it flows westward by the church toward a valley, beyond which the world of the White Mountains rises into view—some of the oldest mountains of this nation—and as I then lift up my eyes to those hills and mountains themselves, especially on a clear fall day, when the bright colors of the maples and the birches and the beeches and the more somber hues of the oaks stand over against the dark figures of the white pines and the hemlocks, I see the grandeur of God.

And more. I rake up all those cuttings from the scything year after year, and wheel them to stack them in large piles near our gardens. In a year or two, this green manure decays into good nutrients for our vegetable garden, where I spread it and dig it in. In this way, the field serves the garden by helping its plants to flourish, along with the other natural nutrients we add to the soil from time to time, like cow manure and green sand. When I lift and push wheelbarrows of cuttings from the pipeline toward our gardens to be composted or when I spread the cow manure or scatter the green sand, and thereafter, in due course, when I kneel down on the earth to weed the vegetable seedlings, I am lifting and pushing and spreading and scattering and weeding in prayer. Because "the earth is the LORD's and the fullness thereof" (Ps 24:1, KJV) and the Lord is there, I believe, in, with, and under not only the grand vistas of the field and the forest and the mountains, but also in, with, and under every furrow of the soil and every glorious green shoot, both the seedlings and the weeds. I am kneeling there on holy ground.

I am particularly grateful for our vegetable garden. Sometimes, scythe in hand, as I catch my breath out on the field, I look across the little stream that runs along the side of the field where I'm working and marvel at that vegetable garden, closer to our house. It has a life of its own, just like the field where I scythe. The growing season in southwestern Maine is short (neighbors still repeat the story of a killer frost in July a hundred and fifty years ago), but after decades of work our soil is good and the fruits of that good earth are usually plentiful.

It's a joy, too, to eat from the garden, in due season. It's akin, for us, to a liturgical calendar. There's the salad season, the zucchini and yellow squash season, the tomato season, the potato season, and the kohl season, each with eating rituals of its own. Fecundity is the word that comes to mind. I have a photograph on my desk of my wife holding a huge armful of chard, half as big as she is. She freezes the harvest of those seasons, as much as she can, and so we eat from our garden virtually the whole year.

I have no illusions that we could get by "living from the land," as some city-folks like to think when they garden in rural areas. But that vegetable garden is nevertheless a gift of unmerited grace. Not the least of such a grace, for us, are the "veggie feasts" that we host for family and friends, three or four times during the growing season. Those feasts, with all their homegrown and home-cooked delicacies covering our table and all the personal warmth around the table, are unmerited grace multiplied. My wife does the cooking and I do the cleaning up when all have gone home. For me, those quiet moments are like the time after the Sunday liturgy, as I've experienced it over many years, when I have washed the chalice and cared for the bread and the wine that remained after that meal and felt the holy silence that enveloped me then.

In this and many other ways, I am ecstatic, often, when I've been contemplating nature at our farmhouse in southwestern Maine. The great Protestant theologian of the last century, Paul Tillich, taught me to use this word in contexts like these. Ecstasy, said Tillich, means "standing outside of yourself." You find yourself, in the midst of your ordinary experience, but standing—or kneeling—on holy ground.

I'm ecstatic all the more so at such times, too, because I often self-consciously see and feel myself as part of larger, interconnected worlds: the ecology of that place in southwestern Maine surely, more particularly the church and its daylilies, of course, and also the rolling field where I scythe and the fructuous vegetable garden where I kneel and my wife's small but elegant perennial garden, celebrating the colors yellow, blue, red, and pink, but then also contemplating beyond in every direction the fragile biosphere which is so preciously layered on this Earth, and the domains of our sun, its solar system, and our galaxy all around us, among the billions and billions of other galaxies—and God, in, with, and under it all, hovering, giving birth to all things as this universe's creative and life-giving Spirit.

2

Cutting through the Ice

CONTEMPLATING THE DEPTHS
BEHIND THE FARMHOUSE

"And just as he was coming up out of the water, he saw the heavens
torn apart and the Spirit descending like a dove on him."

(MARK 1:10)

Late in the fall, my wife and I typically shut down our Maine farmhouse.
We're not skiers, but even if we were, it would be folly for us to keep water in
the pipes of our porous nineteenth-century summer home during the bitter
winter months. We once rented out the place for the winter, and the pipes
froze all the time, even with the furnace on and the woodstove blazing. Still,
two or three times during the winter months we do travel up to that frigid
house for two or three days. Sometimes I wonder why.

It's all the more puzzling when I reflect about what we have to do in
order to travel there and what we have to do while we're there, simply to
maintain ourselves. Our Prius barely handles the narrow, up-and-down
rural roads, covered as they often are with snow and ice. Once we arrive, I
have to chop my way some twenty feet to the front door through iced-over
drifts. Then we lug in not only our modest provisions, but a half-dozen
gallons of water for drinking and cooking. As soon as possible, we begin

to burn precious stacks of firewood lavishly in our Franklin Stove, around which we huddle. First thing the next morning, it's time for me to cut a hole in the ice out back.

We have to use the toilet while we're there, of course, but there's no way to flush it during the winter. No water in the pipes. To address that challenge, I put on my boots, grab hold of a long-handled, flat-edged spade, a small plastic pitcher, and a couple of buckets. I then crunch my way through the deep snow behind the house for a hundred feet or so to a tiny stream that's totally covered by high drifts. Precariously, I inch my way down the almost indiscernible bank of that stream to the underlying ice, maybe two inches thick. Once balanced, I use my spade as an icepick to chop a foot square opening. Then I hunker down over that opening, and contemplate the water that flows there, maybe eight inches deep, moving along even when the temperature has dropped below zero. It must be a comic apparition, were anyone to witness it. There I hover, pitcher in hand, the wind-chill raging around me, bailing out water from beneath the ice, in order to fill the two buckets I've brought with me.

Witness me, then, cautiously carrying a single bucket of nearly frozen water through the snowpack to the back door of our house. Then I repeat the process. Once, by the time I arrived at the house with the second bucket, a skin of new ice had already formed on the first. Even when the sun is beaming down, the ferocious winter temperatures rule the day, and permeate to my hands through my double-lined gloves. All this, so that we can flush the toilet when we need to.

But why? Why not remain at home in our well-heated condominium in the Boston area and warmly continue to embrace our comfortable, retired existence? Why push ourselves, in this way, to confront the elements?

Yes, there's something to be said about this kind of "cozy" experience in Maine, as a friend once suggested: times when "the weather outside is frightful, but the fire is so delightful." There's something to be said about "getting away from it all," no matter where you live. There's something to be said about what one historian of American culture once called, perhaps sardonically, "the quest for contentment in 'the bourgeois interior.'" Be that as it may, why Maine in the winter for us?

One of the factors, on my part, could be my years. Past eighty now, am I secretly regarding myself as some kind of wilderness warrior? Is this an old-age rite or even some masculine thing, to show myself that "I can still do it"? But I think it's more than stereotypical posturing.

Could the real lure of this adventure, for me at least, be that experience of chopping through the ice and seeing the moving water underneath? What do I see? Even though the stream is only eight inches deep, I'm overcome by an experience of what Paul Tillich called "the dimension of depth."

My God! In chilling midwinter, underneath all those drifts and thick ice, reality is moving. See it! Contemplate it! It's flowing. It's going somewhere. We don't live entombed in a world destined for nothing but ice, at the cosmic end of all things. Underneath it all, Being is Becoming, not Stasis.

Granted, this particular encounter with the Depths is only twelve inches square and eight inches deep! But it's a revelation for me when I chop through the ice, under those arctic conditions, to discover that flowing water. To some passerby, it might look odd. It feels odd. Still, I now regard myself, when I stand there, as contemplating ultimate mysteries.

This is how I arrived this ostensibly comical spiritual conclusion. Once, on a family outing to celebrate my daughter-in-law's graduation from a master's program at Dartmouth College, I found occasion to wander through that institution's art museum. There I encountered, for the first time, works by the contemporary Finish-American painter, Eric Aho. Many of his striking abstract impressionistic works depict three-by-four foot squares cut through eight-inch ice near the edge of a sizeable, snow-covered pond. The explanation: those squares in the thick ice depict an opening into which someone who has just come from the sauna can plunge.

Aho enlisted a carpenter and the help of some Finnish friends to construct a sauna by a pond on some land he owns in New Hampshire. There, in the midst of winter, Aho himself cuts the body-sized square openings in the ice with a nineteenth century saw that he purchased from a farmer in Vermont. Aho's own father, a builder of saunas, had as a matter of course grown up deeply shaped by the sauna experience and its traditions in Finland.

Aho began his striking "Ice Cuts" series several years after the New Hampshire sauna had been completed. He is well aware of the near-mythic character of these paintings. The Curator of the exhibit tells us in her introduction to the exhibit that Aho "has observed that for some viewers the ice cut is something that attracts; for others it can be frightening in its empty darkness. It can either evoke the voice of the grave . . . or reflect the infinity of the yellow arctic sky."[5] This creative tension might well be occasioned by Aho's efforts to hold the figural and the nonrepresentational together, which he thinks of as "the collision of realism and abstraction."[6]

The Curator is eager to highlight the power of abstraction in these works. She keeps calling attention to the paintings' lines, colors, shapes, and contrasts. I kept thinking about their spiritual power, a response reminiscent of the aforementioned observers who contemplated these paintings in terms either of death or of life, repulsion or attraction.

Notice the elemental experience suggested by the image of the sauna and the plunge into the waters. I know that experience only second-hand. But it appears to be powerful, almost too much to describe. For some, I understand, the sauna experience can almost be a kind of addiction. They find themselves driven to participate in that ritual, in the quest perhaps for a kind of ecstasy, which they cannot readily understand.

A friend of mine, who lives in Minnesota, describes his encounters with the sauna over the years this way: "*After running out of the hot sauna, your naked body steaming in the below-zero weather, only wearing socks to keep your feet from sticking to the ice, you jump into the hole in the ice (don't think about it—just do it—thinking is a problem at that point), dip under the water surface two or three times and then climb up the wood ladder leaning against the far edge of the rectangular hole. You always do this in pairs so that another set of hands is there to grab you and pull you out in case you panic or somehow end up under the ice. Alas, because of my stents I no longer can do this. Now I tend the fire, sit in the sauna, but can only go out and stand on the small deck of the sauna and let my body steam away the heat until I am cool enough to head back into the sauna. You actually don't feel cold when you go into the water—just your body feeling pin prickles and the sucking sound when you try to breathe as you dip under the surface of the water.*"[7]

Aho surely had that kind of experience in mind and heart as he produced those paintings. But consciously or unconsciously, it appeared to me, he was also exploring much more than that elemental sauna experience itself. Most of the icy water-squares in this exhibit were dark, although one was a bright yellow, as if reflecting sunlight. I found this series gripping, even overwhelming, a testimony to ultimate meanings, a witness to Darkness and to Light. In this respect, I think, I remain a student of Tillich.

Tillich would have celebrated the deeper meanings of those paintings. For Tillich, there is a darkness, a mystery, even a danger to our world: Being and Becoming are threatened by Non-Being, yet, for him, not without moments of mystical ecstasy. Tillich believed—and often demonstrated—that art can reveal those dynamics, that art more generally is a matter of what he called "ultimate concern," not just a matter of images, colors, contrasts, and lines, however striking they might be configured in any given work.

Especially these paintings! The Curator tends to downplay the sauna experience that's presupposed by the artist himself. But don't these paintings suggest death and resurrection? More particularly, could they not also be alluding to the image of Jesus himself coming up out of the water of the Jordan when he was baptized, with the heavens above being ripped apart and the Spirit descending on him then and there in the midst of those waters? If these paintings were not intended at some level to suggest these particular themes concerning Jesus, might they not still be alluding to *the believer's* dying and rising with Christ? Surely, in my view, they do suggest some kind of primal death and rebirth from the womb of the Depths, and possibly more.

I have concluded that that's the vision that claims me, as I chop through that thick ice on that little stream behind our Maine farmhouse. It's a matter of ultimate concern. It's a matter of death and life. In biblical terms, it's a matter of dying with Christ and rising with the one who himself emerged from the waters full of the Spirit. It's a matter of my own mundane experience being ripped apart, and the Spirit taking hold of me in recollection of Jesus' baptism in the Jordan. In Tillich's terms, I'm grasped by the power of Being overcoming Non-Being, Life overcoming Death. That's the underlying reason, doubtless among others, I have decided, why I keep wanting us to undertake those winter excursions, so that I can cut through that ice to contemplate those Depths, strangely perhaps, but for me ecstatically.

3

Taking a Plunge in the Niagara River

INTIMATIONS OF A BAPTISMAL MYSTICISM

"Jesus answered, 'Very truly, I tell you, no one can enter the kingdom
of God without being born of the water and the Spirit.'"

(JOHN 3:5)

I grew up in the Buffalo, New York, area, not far from Niagara Falls. Lake
Erie was very much part of that world, and I was very much aware of it from
an early age. I was drawn to that lake often as a young boy.

Sadly, in recent years this magnificent body of fresh water has been
poisoned by a thick, vast and growing coat of toxic algae, covering a sixth of
its surface and bringing with it a huge dead zone at its lower levels, reducing
fish populations drastically. These developments also make large portions
of the lake inaccessible for recreational use. Sadly, too, a 2013 study found
that Western New York (infamous in the past for the poisonous Love Ca-
nal) is home to some 800 hazardous waste sites that could wreak environmental havoc in Lake Erie and possibly other Great Lakes, too, in years to
come. But things were different when I first got acquainted with that lake.
For me, back then, it was a charged experience just to stand at its edge and
to contemplate those majestic fresh waters, now and again skipping rocks
over the near surface, as young boys often do.

My grandparents owned a summer home, almost at the edge of that lake, and from there I would walk down to the lake and wander around its beaches and inlets. When I was a college student, I worked one summer for Bethlehem Steel, right at the edge of the lake. My family also took week-long cruises on Lake Erie and, beyond, on all the Great Lakes, all the way to greatest of them all, Lake Superior, which gave me still broader perspectives on those waters. But it was the easterly egress of Lake Erie that fascinated me the most in my early years, as its waters poured into the Niagara River, propelled themselves toward and over the magnificent thundering of Niagara Falls, then through the towering and gaping Niagara River gorge, and on into Lake Ontario.

Living as close to the Falls as my family did, we visited them often, this, because they were such an astounding sight in themselves, but also because friends and family members from around the country found that our home was a convenient station on *their* way to visit the Falls. When I was a teenager, in the midst of the sometimes oppressive summer heat, my friends and I would on occasion jump into someone's car and head for the Niagara River. Our destination was halfway between Lake Erie and the Falls. But we thought of the Falls intensely, nevertheless, as we would plunge into the surging river waters far above the Falls, to see if we could make any headway swimming upstream. We couldn't.

We were, of course, horrified by the thought of being carried too far downstream. Images of helpless human bodies, being swept along by the torrents and then over the Falls, flowed around in our minds. But it was safe enough for us, all of whom were accomplished swimmers, as we flailed our arms at the height of our powers against the currents, only to remain stationary. In retrospect, I think that that swimming was a kind of—safe—adolescent dancing with death. I still remember the shock I felt the first time I jumped into those cold, raging currents.

All the more so, I was fascinated with the Falls and never tired going there. Who can describe Niagara Falls, this icon of the historic American consciousness? Many writers and countless painters have tried. I will only tell what little I know. The Falls were formed at the end of the last ice age. Waters from three of the bodies we now call the Great Lakes carved out these Falls, leaving the gigantic river gorge before them, as those waters made their way forward, eventually, toward the Atlantic Ocean and as those waters relentlessly chiseled away at the bedrock underneath, inching the Falls ever closer back toward Lake Erie.

Today, over the two separate branches of the Falls, the American and the Canadian, more than six million cubic feet of water fall every minute. They plunge over heights that reach as high as 170 feet and they extend more than a half-mile wide. Thundering is indeed a good word to describe the impression they make when you stand there on the observation platform, feet away from the apex of the Falls. My brother remembers feeling the ground tremble under his feet at that point, on the Canadian side, when he stood there as a boy. Sometimes, looking down from that point, he and I would watch a little ship, far below in the gorge, often obscured by the mist—it was called the "Maid of the Mist" in those days—making its way toward the Falls, with yellow-coated tourists packed on its decks, and then turning around, just in time, it seemed to me.

Often, when my family had visitors and when we had motored down to see the Falls, after we had come home I would go to bed at night, astounded. I would lie there thinking: never mind whether *I* am awake or asleep, *those tons and tons of water* keep flowing over the Falls and keep carving out the gorge in front of them without ceasing! It was truly an awe-inspiring memory for me, as I lay there in the solitude of my bed, falling asleep.

Once, as a young man, Paul Tillich, who, after he emigrated to the U.S., was to become one of the nation's leading theologians during the middle of the twentieth century, visited a steel mill in his native Prussia. It was my privilege to study six years with Tillich, already as an undergraduate. This was a story he told more than once, in my hearing. I am not sure whether he ever wrote about it. With youthful passion and spiritual abandon, so he recounted, he looked at the flowing molten steel and said, "That is God." Tillich would later qualify such statements carefully. But I know what he had meant. Had I had the same kind of inspiration in my own youth, I easily could have looked at the Falls, in particular, and could have said likewise, "That is God."

On the other hand, with Tillich, had I made that kind of a statement, I surely would have wanted to revise it later in my life, after I had studied some theology and had more clearly understood the importance of affirming God's transcendence as well as God's immanence. But in those youthful years, Lake Erie and the Niagara River and its Falls and its gorge were spiritually overpowering for me. In retrospect, I think that what was claiming me then, as it claims my heart and soul today, was what I now think of as my baptismal mysticism.

Baptism was a major event in churches like the one in which I was received as an infant, Resurrection Lutheran Church in Buffalo. As I now see things in retrospect, Baptism was celebrated robustly in such churches, both in the life of the infant's family and in the life of the congregation of which that family was a member. And not just for ceremonial reasons. Whether they could readily find the words to say it, the members of such congregations knew in their bones that a Baptism was much more than a name-giving or the mere celebration of the birth of a healthy child or a way of doting on the cuteness of a baby. They firmly believed, or many of them did, that some profoundly gracious and irrevocably lifelong transaction between God and the child, and the community of faith, was being established by the sacrament of Baptism, with the water and with God's word of promise. They deeply understood, most of them, that Baptism was the way, for them, to enter the Kingdom of God, by being born of the water and the Spirit.

I grew up with that heritage, and then I found it enriched in my seminary years when I was exposed to the baptismal theology of the patriarch of the tradition according to whose canons I myself had been baptized, the sixteenth-century Protestant Reformer, Martin Luther. Luther had a profound sense for the immediacy of God in nature. Yes, for Luther, nature was a *mask* of God (*larva Dei*), but it was surely for him also a mask *of God*. For Luther, God was deeply and pervasively "in, with, and under" the world of nature. For Luther, nature was not quite, in so many words, "the theater of God's glory" as it was for Luther's fellow Protestant reformer, John Calvin. Nor was it the world revealed by the ecstatic visions of the modern Jesuit poet Gerard Manley Hopkins, for whom the whole creation is "charged with the grandeur of God." Still, for Luther, nature was astoundingly permeated, through and through, with the powerful presence of God. If you truly were to understand a grain of wheat, Luther once observed, you would die of wonder.

Strikingly, Luther gave voice to that same kind of profound sense for the presence of God in nature when the reformer talked about Baptism. For him, the very God who is in, with, and under all things is also revealingly and graciously present in the waters of Baptism. In those waters, when God's word of promise is spoken, according to Luther, God discloses God-self not just as an immediate and powerful presence, but all the more so as a self-giving, gracious, and faithful presence. For Luther, these two themes,

God in nature generally and God in Baptism particularly, are thoroughly and inseparably wedded.

Such thoughts sometimes percolate to my own consciousness, when in the fall I'm scything in rural Maine or contemplating a little stream in the winter under two inches of ice back of our family farmhouse in the same locale. The God whom I encounter when I'm contemplating nature is for me, as a matter of course, the very God in whose name I once was baptized.

I am telling a story here, not making an argument. That's the way I have experienced water and water-Baptism for many years. Only recently, as a matter of fact, in these my older years, have I settled on some kind of conceptuality in order to try to interpret my longstanding spiritual experience with water in general and with Baptism in particular.

The terminology may sound odd, but it makes sense to me. As I have reflected about my own experience, such as I have been aware of it, I have discovered *a bifocal spirituality* (in the sense of two foci). On the one hand, there's what might be called my sacramental encounter with nature. On the other hand, there's my personal and my pastoral experience with the sacrament of Baptism. More about the latter in a moment.

In Luther's language, it has dawned on me—or I have gradually been made aware—that God is in, with, and under Lake Erie, the Niagara River and its Falls, and that God is in, with, an under the waters of Baptism. And more. Recalling that chilling and ominous plunge into the Niagara River not all that far upriver from the Falls helps me to grasp the meaning of dying and rising with Christ in Baptism.

I know that some Christians, not to speak of those who are struggling to decide whether the Christian faith might be an option for them, may well be perplexed with these intimations of my Baptismal mysticism, if not dumfounded. If you are one of these, be assured that I fully understand. But I wonder whether the Church has failed you in this respect, if not in others. You may immediately relate to my narrative about plunging into the Niagara River, but you may find it difficult, perhaps impossible, even to begin to understand how I can think of Baptism with the same kind of spiritual intensity. Many serious souls these days will say precisely this, that God is more real for them along the rocky coast of Maine or on a wilderness trek in the Rockies than during the Sunday morning liturgy.

And Baptism? I fault our churches. If Baptism is positioned at the edges of the Church's life, as it sometimes is, and if Baptism in practice—although not in the mind of the baptizing priest or pastor—has become little more than a happy time for the larger family to celebrate the arrival of a new baby, to adore that newborn, and to get out their smart phones to take photos, then why bother? But it doesn't need to be that way.

Enter a radically new idea, which is as old as the early Church and as familiar as historic American Baptist churches, both white and black. Those American churches have taught many Christians of many denominations to sing "Shall We Gather at the River?" That was not merely a metaphor for earliest Christians and those old-time American Christians. They actually *did* gather at the river. Which is why a recent proposal by a Lutheran theologian is so traditional, even while it may sound so radical to many inside our mainline churches.

Lisa Dahill has argued that *all* Baptisms—wherever possible, depending on the weather and other variables like that—should be *outdoors*.[8] I had sympathetic labor pains, as it were, when I first heard Dahill lecture about this topic.

My son and his wife once asked me to baptize first one of my grandsons and then the second outdoors at our farmhouse in Maine, which I did one summer and then another summer two years later. This is a story I eagerly want to narrate. But first let me tell you about me and Baptism more generally, over the years.

I'm not sure about how other priests and pastors feel about baptizing, but I suspect that I'm not alone in this: during the course of more than four decades as a practicing pastor, I was deeply moved, spiritually ecstatic, every time I was privileged to preside over a Baptism. Lutherans like me, actually, tend to go overboard on this. We typically read—or, better, incant—Luther's great and extended "Flood Prayer," which proclaims all the marvelous works of God with and through water, from the waters of chaos in the originating moments of the creation to the flood story of Noah and finally to the Baptism of Jesus by John in the Jordan. And then we baptize with water, profusely, many of us. Over the years, when that overpowering moment arrived, I was almost always at the edge of tears.

But now consider such an experience—*outdoors*. True, I would as a matter of course have been deeply moved when I baptized *my own* grandsons, no matter where I was. Still, imagine the setting. At our farmhouse, surrounded by native flowers in what we call our Hidden Garden, next to a profusion of rose blossoms and great honeysuckle bushes in bloom, refracted in some shade from several towering ash trees, and caressed by a warm summer breeze in the sunshine, how could we all not be ecstatic?!

Then there was the baptismal water, many gallons of it in a large white crockery container, the kind that some gardeners use for planting trees on patios. The water in that huge vessel came from our drilled well, from three-hundred-and-sixty-nine feet down in the bedrock. We had pumped the water earlier in the day so that it could be warmed by the sun.

There I took hold of my grandsons in their nakedness, on two different occasions, and plunged them totally underwater, three times. At that moment, each time, everyone of course gasped. I am happy to report that both infants came through those near-death experiences alive and screaming. Such is the visual power and the charged meaning of Baptism, or such it can be, in a rich outdoor setting, with abundant waters, a world of many-splendored colors, and vibrant sunshine. We had invited as many friends as we could possibly persuade to attend. They all formed a large circle around the baptismal action and were, of course, swept up by the joy of that moment. They cheered each time, after I had baptized one of my grandsons. Some wept, along with the babies.

Your local church can claim just that kind of experience, if it has the imagination. The best case, of course, is to go down to the river or to the lake (if the quality of the water and other issues like safety permits that). The officiating priest or pastor will go into the waters, taking that plunge, leading or—in the case of infant Baptism—carrying the one being baptized. The officiating priest or pastor will have spoken of God's presence in those waters and of how the one to be baptized—whether infant or adult—is about to go down into God's presence, there to die with Christ and there to rise from those depths to new life with Christ, then and forever. The officiating priest or pastor will also have spoken about how precious water is for us humans, what a blessing it is when it is pure and abundant, that our very bodies are mostly water and that we're descended from the fish of the sea, but that, sadly, water all around the world in our time is groaning in travail, due to human greed and malfeasance. But that bad news will never be the last word, the officiant will have announced.

Members of the whole congregation—for Baptism must be communal whenever that is humanly possible—will have been invited right at the start to take off their shoes, as Lisa Dahill once invited a congregation of which I was a part during a liturgy in Ohio that was celebrated at the edge of a small stream: to feel God's good earth on which we walk, to know by touch the goodness of our own earthly bodies, and to remember, astoundingly, that in Baptism the church celebrates God's promise, not just for the one being baptized, but for the whole Earth and, indeed, for the whole cosmos.

Could that river or that lake or that stream come alive for that congregation? Could all those gathered there experience that water charged with the presence and the promise of God? Could they find themselves overwhelmed at that moment by what some might later choose to call their own baptismal mysticism? Could they learn at that moment that contemplating nature need not just be an experience of respectful and wondering distance: that it can be a moment of engagement, of taking the plunge, not standing apart, even an experience of being graciously embraced by the God who dwells in, with, and under the whole world of nature? Could they not learn, more particularly, that that's what being born of water and the Spirit can mean?

4

Walking along the Charles River

WITNESSING SIGNS OF THE KINGDOM

"Jesus answered them, 'Go and tell John what you hear and see:
the blind receive their sight, the lame walk, the lepers are cleansed,
the deaf hear, the dead are raised, and the poor have the good news
brought to them.'"

(MATT 11:4–5)

Following the example of the American transcendentalist Henry David
Thoreau, my wife and I have become habitual walkers in recent years, although much more modestly than the Concord, Massachusetts, sage and
at some distance from his beloved Walden Pond. One particular route,
however, has taken on visionary proportions in my own soul, akin to the
intensity of Thoreau's experience with walking, although quite different in
character.

The two of us often saunter along the banks of the now rejuvenated
Charles River between Cambridge and Boston, Massachusetts. Its pollution
a public scandal for decades, the river has been dramatically cleaned up
in recent years, so much so that the "Charles River Swimming Club" held
its first-ever open swimming race in 2007 in order to boost that group's

continuing campaign in behalf of the river. Along the north bank where we walk, there are hidden wooded places where one can remove oneself, somewhat, from the urban setting of cosmopolitan Cambridge. In addition to the wonderful commonplace—the doves, the flickers, the robins, the ducks, the geese, and the seagulls—we have seen the extraordinary: a loon diving and then emerging many moments later to swallow a fish in a gulp; red-tailed hawks soaring high above; an elegant Great Blue Heron standing still in some rushes at the bank; and even, in one halcyon moment, two gracious white swans gliding majestically up the river.

A mélange of people also engage the river happily during the warmer seasons—students in rowing shells, early and late in the day; families in canoes, mostly on weekends; solitary souls in kayaks at virtually any time. On the south bank of the river you can contemplate many spacious grassy spaces and an abundance of shade trees where, on a typical early summer's evening, you can walk in the midst of strollers and joggers and cyclists and those who have come to fish, to picnic, to play, to garden in civic plots, or to harvest mulberries.

Along the way, you can hear a symphony of tongues, what I take to be Spanish, Russian, Haitian, Vietnamese, Armenian, Chinese, and English, among others. The members of this improbable congregation are many-colored and of all ages and social classes. People smile at each other and give every appearance of feeling safe and being content. They seem to look after each other, too. On one occasion, when I was doing one of my elderly "power walks," a man about my age, who was sitting on a park bench with a young girl, who must have been his granddaughter, hollered over to me as I labored by: "You're doing fine! Don't get discouraged!" All this appears to me to be a world of peace, in the biblical sense of *shalom*, replete with cultural diversity, a sense of spiritual well-being, respectful mutuality, physical security, a welcoming of all the generations, and contemplation of a natural world that has at least some measure of its own life, free of human intervention.

When I embark on such walks myself, I often have one regular destination, the Episcopal monastery on the north side of the river, one of the homes of the Society of Saint John the Evangelist, which came to Cambridge in 1870. There I am blessed to be able to kneel in prayer any day during the week and often to participate in moving liturgies, like the Great Vigil of Easter Eve, in the gracious 1936 basilica-style Chapel of St. Mary and St. John, whose massive but elegant granite structure commands the riverfront at that point. That the chapel's inner, mammoth wood roof beams were once part of a bridge over Boston's Mystic River only heightens my own fascination with the charged spiritual and liturgical drama that daily emerges in its midst and deepens my own engagement with its Charles River setting all the more.

That pilgrimage through those different places—the worlds of the loons and the swans, of the ordinary folks of many nations at peace, and of the community of faith gathered in hope for its Eucharist and other rites— is for me a kind of mundane mystical journey. For me, the worlds of the still, wild woods and the people's park and the quiet, yet songful basilica all inform each other inseparably, and all bespeak God's presence and the promises of God for the whole creation. When I contemplate nature, as I often do, it is always—implicitly, if not explicitly—in moments that are variegated pieces sewn into the grand quilt of God's infinitely complex history with all things.

It so happens that I also read the witness of the Scriptures in a like manner, as celebrating that grand quilt. This is no accident, because the liturgy, after all, hands me the Scriptures every week, and has done so ever since my parents promised at my Baptism to put those Scriptures into my hands. This they did chiefly by their devout participation in the liturgy, with me and my siblings in tow when we were children, which impressed me enormously. Now when I read those Scriptures, I encounter that very vision of God's will for our world: nature, human community, and church in differentiated but interwoven harmony, with the church called to celebrate and to embody the vision of divine *shalom*, of peace with justice, which is God's ultimate purpose—which is to say, God's *eschatological* purpose—for the whole universe. The biblical promise of God's last things (*ta eschata* in Greek, hence our word *eschatology*) and the inreach of those last things into the present moment has been very real for me, for many years.

I use the much-abused language of eschatology here, because it is so important to me. Hence, I will try to be as clear as I possibly can be. I am not talking here about being "raptured" up to heaven with a few other believers, there to await the destruction of the Earth. On the contrary, in the Bible the city of God comes down to Earth (Rev 21:2) to be established in the midst of "a new heaven and a new earth" (Rev 21:1). Nor do I have access to any kind of timetable for the arrival of that new city in the midst of that new heaven and new earth. That is not for us to know, as the Bible also says (Acts 1:7).

Eschatology is the witness to the future arrival of the consummated creation, when God will be all in all (1 Cor 15:28), a thought that I can give voice to only with hesitation, since now if we see that future of God at all, we only "see through a glass darkly" (1 Cor 13:12, KJV). On the other hand, that future of God has arrived and does arrive on Earth ahead of time, as it were. Paradoxically, it arrives before it arrives, finally. It arrives powerfully in the life, death, and resurrection of Jesus Christ, and then, mediated through him by the power of the Spirit, in the life of the church, which is the body of Christ. The future of God arrives here and now, when it does, as a "foretaste." The technical theological language is that that future of God arrives "proleptically."

All this is a deep mystery. In faith and in hope, sinful mortals like we who are members of Christ's body believe we can live, by the inspiration of the Holy Spirit, in that future world here and now. Indeed, with the eyes of faith and hope given to us in the body of Christ we believe that we can contemplate signs of that future world, as our eyes are illuminated by the Spirit, now and again, around us. This is the faith and this is the hope that, when it is so given to me, leads me to see those many fragmentary signs of *shalom* as I walk along the Charles River. These, to be sure, are not the particular revelatory signs that Jesus called the disciples of John the Baptist to ponder, the blind receiving their sight, the lame walking, the lepers being cleansed, the deaf hearing, the dead being raised, and the poor hearing the good news of the Gospel hope. But they're not altogether different either. They are, for me, scintillating: sparks (*scintilla*) that reflect the brilliantly revelatory signs of the Kingdom that Jesus himself announces.

Be assured, however. I am well aware that when I saunter along that river, alone or with my wife, I am contemplating the world through rose-colored glasses. Or, better, in the apt image of John Calvin, I am seeing the world through biblical lenses, which I have been taught to use in the community of faith and hope. This means that I am seeing the world primarily in terms of its divine promise, to be consummated when the end of all things arrives, when the day of the new heavens and the new earth, in which righteousness dwells, dawns, as announced by the church's Bible. The world I see reflects "the last things" of God's purposes, a vision given to me in fragments as one who partakes in the body of Christ, here and now.

But the actual world where I walk is not only a world that offers us scintilla of eschatological peace, here and now: it is also a world that is thoroughly broken and pervasively polluted and rampant with violence.

On some hot summer days, the Charles River may be permeated with an explosive growth of an algae that can be highly toxic to humans and animals, in response to which authorities suspend all boating, which casts the idea of swimming in the river into serious doubt. Along the shores of the river, Japanese knotweed, an invasive, bamboo-like perennial that forms dense thickets, is choking the life out of many native plants. Such occurrences remind us that the interconnectedness of our earth has sometimes deadly dimensions, as it responds to the stresses and strains of our time.

A fenced-in, gone-wild acre that I pass at one point in my walk once held a military arsenal's storage area; years ago, it leeched toxic chemicals into the river and is still off-limits to the public. The terrors of war come to mind every time I notice it. Moreover, one dare not walk along the Charles unguardedly at night for fear of assaults. So the rejuvenated river itself and its sometimes peaceful environs is by no means that ultimate river that flows through the City of God, for which we Christians long when we sing, "Shall We Gather at the River?"

Further, I am very much aware that even an imperfectly restored Charles River is unusual today, compared to many rivers of the world, depleted or poisoned as they are. I understand that a peaceful, multiethnic, multigenerational, and multiclass early-evening stroll in a riverside park is today an exception compared to the experience of most of the people around the globe whose early evenings are filled violence, strife, and hunger. I know that even quiet prayers or an exquisite liturgy in a gracious chapel can mask ecclesial corruption—painfully apparent in recent years to those of us who live in the Boston area, where stories of priestly sexual abuse seem to know no end.

In such a world, dominated by the principalities and powers of Darkness, I am compelled to ask: how can I sustain that eschatological hope that so enchants my soul? How can anyone? These questions are constantly on my mind and in my heart, as I find myself carried away contemplating reflections and refractions of the Kingdom in ordinary encounters with people and with nature along the Charles.

5

From Lake Wobegon to the Streets of Manhattan

BEHOLD THEN FOLLOW

"And he said to them, 'Follow me.'"

(MATT 4:19)

Behold the lilies, said Jesus. He also said many other things, of course. If I were to imagine him saying only *two* things, however, it would be this: "Behold the lilies, then follow me." Behold the beauty of that holiness, then come with me and be holy. For Jesus, contemplation and discipleship are inseparable.

Such thoughts percolated in my mind as I found myself sitting in the middle of 52nd Street in Manhattan on the pavement, waiting for our street-full of a thousand or so stationary "marchers" to join with countless others, already underway, on Sunday, September 21, 2014 during the Peoples Climate March. A street vendor was tip-toeing in and around the crowd seated on the blacktop, trying to persuade men to purchase a rose or two for "their ladies." Flowers! Just what we all needed.

But of course we did. Never mind the "flower children" of the nineteen-sixties. We all must be flower children these days, I thought to myself. How are you going to behold the lilies, if there aren't any lilies anymore?

Then there are the fireflies. When our children were young, we would sometimes get out a blanket when we were in Maine, and just sit there on the grass some evenings watching the fireflies amassed in brilliant clouds, hovering just above the back field. Now the fireflies are gone, by and large. The same is true for the barn swallows that used to flourish in and around the chimney of the church next door to our Maine house. They're gone. My wife and I imagine, too, that over the course of forty plus years in Maine we have experienced not only a silent spring, as Rachel Carson once did, but also a silent summer and a silent fall. As we sit on our screened-in porch, at various times during the year, we sometimes ask ourselves, where have all the birds gone? Of course, we hear some of their songs. But the sounds of silence can sometimes be depressing.

With that flower vendor moving out of sight and with nothing else to think about, it soon dawned on me that I was once again falling into an environmental funk. That's a constant temptation of ecological theologians such as myself, along with many other people of good will these days. Rather, heed the words of somebody's grandmother, who once said: better to light a candle than to curse the darkness.

Having rid my soul of that environmental funk, I then found myself slipping into a theological funk. It occurred to me that I was part of a small contingent of Lutherans. I was *a Lutheran protester*?! An oxymoron, if I ever heard one (Martin Luther himself was something else, of course). I knew this story all too well.

I wrote my undergraduate honors thesis on the German resistance to Hitler. There wasn't much, I concluded. Yes, the Resistance Movement itself was remarkable and, all the more so, the life and death of the German Lutheran Pastor, Dietrich Bonhoeffer, whom I discussed at great length in my thesis. But as soon as I began to do research about such matters, I learned that many, if not most, German Lutherans simply stepped out of the way as the Nazi Behemoth clambered on toward absolute power. Some Lutherans even cheered that Behemoth. Whether Lutherans in the U.S. have been much better, I'm not totally convinced. Historically, my own ecclesial Lutheran identity, born of rebellion by a Catholic monk, had not pushed *me* in the direction of protest, at least when I was growing up. I knew in my blood, in those days, that Lutherans after the time of Luther weren't given to protesting too much. But as I looked around me at my fellow Lutherans sitting on the blacktop with me, my theological funk began to subside, as I realized that something relatively new was going on here.

36

It must have been Garrison Keillor who observed that at the gates of heaven the Jews will carry a shofar, the Catholics a crucifix, and the Lutherans a bowl of Jello. I saw signs of that Lutheran sensibility on the streets of Manhattan that morning, all around me. Nevertheless I celebrated that particular spiritual presence—in the form that I observed it at that moment.

Just about every group that I saw carried its own sign or banner or flag, announcing its identity and its presence and promoting its own commitment to this good cause: the Hare Krishnas, the Unitarians, the Service Employees International Union, 350.org, the Sierra Club, the Hindus, the Women's International League for Peace and Freedom, St. John's Sunday School, Harlem, and many more.

We Lutherans carried three-by-two foot green signs, with "Climate Justice: For All of God's Creation" in large letters. In tiny print, I mean really tiny print, down in the corner of our signs, I spied some other letters. If you held the sign close to your eyes, as if you were reading a newspaper, you could identify these words, "Evangelical Lutheran Church in America." Onlookers might well have wondered: who *are* those creation-justice people with those bright green signs?

I gently chided one of the Lutheran staff workers about this, a young woman from the church's advocacy office in the nation's capital. It turned out that she had had a hand in designing our signs. "It never crossed my mind," she said, "to put 'Lutherans' in big letters. We were looking for the distinct message we wanted to convey, and we thought that 'Climate Justice for All God's Creation' was it." I agreed. Bless her. Good Lutherans always strive to announce the Truth, never to announce themselves!

On the face of it, that approach makes sense. After all, as far as I could tell, there were fewer than a hundred self-identifying Lutherans participating in that march of some 310,000 souls. And *we* were then to make a big deal about *our* identity?! Be that as it may, I was proud (a non-Lutheran sentiment, I know) to be carrying my own modest sign. Why? Because we had got it right. We had left Lake Wobegon behind and had headed for the streets of Manhattan. With that thought, I felt that I was emerging from my theological funk. But not totally.

There are Lutherans and then there are Lutherans, of course. To be perfectly honest, I prefer to hang out with Lutherans like those sitting there on the pavement around me, whose Jello had been spiked with the energy drink of *discipline*. For me, this is a critically important theological point for my own Wobegone identity as I aspire to be a follower of Jesus in this, our era of planetary emergency. Let me explain.

Martin Luther held that people coming together can be identified as "church," that is, as followers of Jesus, when two things are evident: *first*, when God's message about Jesus (God's Word) is truly taught and powerfully proclaimed; and, *second*, when the sacraments of the Church, above all Baptism and the Eucharist, are celebrated in a way that is faithful to that message.

John Calvin taught the same, but he *added* a third "mark of the Church," *discipline*. For Calvin, you can identify a group of people as Christians when, in addition to their faithful preaching and their faithful administration of the sacraments, they *also* exhibit signs that they are taking up their crosses to follow Jesus. In the words of that simple—some would say simplistic—hymn that was popular in the Christian counterculture during the nineteen-sixties in North America: "You will know that we are Christians by our love." Calvin's rendering of this point was much more sophisticated than my own interpretation here, as was Luther's, but I think that the basic contrast I've drawn between the two Reformers' views is correct.

Of more importance to me here, however, is this fateful theological fact. Calvin's notion that the signs of the true Church are three—Word and Sacrament *and* discipline—was taken up in a fresh way, whether self-consciously depending on Calvin I do not know, by Dietrich Bonhoeffer. This is what Bonhoeffer's famous book, *The Cost of Discipleship*, was all about.[9] If you don't have discipleship, Bonhoeffer argued, you end up with what he called "cheap grace." This kind of theological understanding of the Church's faith then propelled Bonhoeffer to become a participant in the plot to kill the tyrant and mass murderer, Adolph Hitler, and eventually led to Bonhoeffer's own death in prison, after that plot had failed.

How different is the situation we face today? It's profoundly different in many ways. Yet there are some wrenching similarities. Climate change, which has been precipitated by the powerful and the wealthy of this world, is causing enormous disruptions of the Earth's ecosystems and of the well-being of the poor of the earth, in keeping with the traditional African saying, "When two elephants fight, it's the grass that suffers." Rising sea levels will soon wreak devastation on the millions of mostly poor people who live in coastal Bangladesh. The exhaustion or poisoning of water resources, especially in places like the Middle East, will in all likelihood devastate vast regions of arable land and set in motion huge migrations of displaced

persons, most of them poor, this, in addition to migrations already underway due to war. Globally, coral reefs are in serious danger, which threatens
the wellbeing not only of a quarter of all marine species, but also the wellbeing of thirty million people around the globe who fish for a living.

Then there is the mundanely measurable, but undoubtedly monstrous, toll that climate change will take on all the creatures of the Earth,
not just humans, but plants and animals and their habitats everywhere. Not
to speak of the desecration of natural beauty all over the planet: the sublime glaciers of Switzerland and Glacier National Park, for example, have
already begun to vanish. Forests are being weakened, many of them dying,
in virtually all regions of the Earth. Even the gracious monarch butterflies
in North America are seriously in trouble.

Extinction may well become *the* code word to describe the horizon
of every earthly creature in decades to come. This clearly is a planetary
emergency of immense proportions, not unlike the European emergency
that Bonhoeffer experienced, when he contemplated the ongoing German
killing of Jews, Gypsies, gays, and the handicapped, the enormous destruction wrought by Nazi aggression more generally, and the prospect of a
subjugation of the whole of Europe to Nazi brute force and perhaps areas
beyond Europe, too.

Not every Christian is called to be a Bonhoeffer, to be sure. But every Christian is surely called to take with utmost seriousness the cost of
discipleship in these times of planetary emergency. It will not do simply to
preach and to administer the sacraments, and then to return to business
as usual in our—to this point—relatively well-protected North American
world. Nor will it do, as American "nature-lovers" are sometimes prone to
do, to travel to wilderness areas, contemplate them in amazement, even see
them as the handiwork of God, and then return to their safe and comfortable urban or suburban walled-in communities. Those who have ears to
hear in this generation will hear that, to adapt an image from the Apostle
Paul, the whole Earth is groaning. And Christians who are committed to
bear the cost of discipleship, ought to be in the middle of many, if not all,
the struggles to respond to that groaning and by laboring to "protect and
serve" the earth (Gen 2:15, author's translation) and all it inhabitants.

What heirs of the Lutheran Reformation are called to do today, I am
convinced, is to join in a new kind of *procession*, with other faith communities which will surely want to take similar steps, predicated on their own
traditions: from Lake Wobegon to the streets of Manhattan. And to do that

Lutherans will have to be trained in a kind of non-violent alterative to the military's training of its Special Forces.

Procession, then, is *the* word for Lutherans—and for other Christians in their own ways—today. Procession is the word for us to juxtapose to extinction. Liturgically we Lutherans know what procession means: recall Sunday's Gospel procession, when the Gospel book is carried, led by the processional Cross, into the midst of the people. Now imagine that procession, once the Gospel has been proclaimed, not returning back to the sanctuary, but turning and heading for the door to the world outside the Church.

The Mass for Creation I attended at 8:45 a.m. the Sunday of the Peoples Climate March at St. Peter's Church, Manhattan, was replete with processions, even though it was a low Mass that day: from the baptismal pool to the Table, from the Table, with the bread and wine, down into the midst of the people, from the pews moving to meet the ministers of the Eucharist, from that whole place of assembly—all together now, passing near the baptismal pool, making the sign of the Cross with the water along the way—to a meeting room, for instructions and coffee, of course. Then we continued processing out into the streets of Manhattan.

St. Peter's does it all the more dramatically during the great Mass of the Easter Vigil. For a segment of the Scripture readings during that high liturgy, the whole congregation processes out of the sanctuary right on to the busy sidewalks of midtown Manhattan on a Saturday night. There, led by a processional Cross, vested clergy, and trumpets, the congregation sings Easter hymns as it marches to each corner of the block, from 54th Street and Lexington Avenue and back again. At each corner the Word of God is announced, with the help of a good electric megaphone.

Let's hear it for the Gospel Procession! Call the Gospel book a bowl of Jello, if you wish. But this is the Truth, typically unheard amidst the noise of our society, but a liberating promise for the crowds that walk such streets at any time or for those undocumented families that pick the apples in Washington State or for those nameless workers who wash the floors and change the linens in the high-rise hotels of Hong Kong or for those Inuit Lutheran parishioners whose families have lived on the island of Shismaref in Alaska for hundreds of generations, for the first time now being flooded by rising ocean currents, which have forced all to vacate their ancient island home.

This is what the Gospel procession announces. It's all going somewhere! There's hope for the whole creation! There's justice, finally, for every creature! It may not look like much now. What's a modest hundred, mostly waspish Lutheran marchers compared to a huge, incredibly diverse 310,000? What's a mere 310,000 climate justice marchers compared to the upwards of 13 million citizens who live in greater New York City and who are often preoccupied with other things? What's a New York City committed to reducing its greenhouse gas emissions 80 percent by 2050 compared to the whole nation of India now planning to add 455 coal-fired plants for electricity in the next five years?

The point is this. Behold then follow. Open the sanctuary doors and get that Gospel procession out on to the streets. Never mind if others think that you're carrying Jello. Never mind if you think that you're in an environmental or even a theological funk. In fact, by faith alone you're carrying the Gospel Truth. There's hope for every creature! That's what we've been called to announce, in the midst of all the other countless and likewise called groups and communities and organizations who also are struggling to care for the good Earth and all its inhabitants.

I saw one sign: "Atheists for Climate Justice." I have no doubt that they were called by God to be there. For us Lutherans and our fellow travelers, I say: whatever else others might be thinking or doing at this moment, start preparing now for the next Peoples Climate March. But without delay, do this: spike your Jello with the energy drink of discipline.

PART 2

Explorations

6

Confronting the Ambiguities of Contemplating Nature

A VIEW FROM DOWN UNDER

"So he told them this parable: 'Which one of you, having a hundred
sheep and losing one of them, does not leave the ninety-nine in the
wilderness and go after the one that is lost until he finds it?'"

(LUKE 15:3–4)

They asked me what I thought. An academic and church consortium
brought me to lovely Adelaide in southern Australia in March of 2015 to
present a paper on ecological theology and spirituality.[10] Along the way
they also asked each of the conferees to take some quiet time of their own
to reflect about his or her own spirituality of nature. I thought to myself:
have I thought about anything else over the last fifty years?! But I did what
I was told.

I found the time for my own reflection when all the other conferees
were off visiting wineries in that, one of Australia's richest wine-producing
regions. I absented myself from that trip, spoilsport that I was, since it was
Lent. And following my simple, if not simple-minded, practice of many
years, I had "given up" imbibing any kind of alcohol during those forty

days. It would have been boring for me, and all the more so for all the others, to go wine-tasting and then not to taste any wine.

Left behind. That was a good setting for reflection. The elegant hotel which was the conference center had once been the site of a winery. But the land in which all those vines grew in that region told a different story. That land, of course, had once been Aboriginal land, an often repressed truth in Australia that the conference planners announced at every opportunity. Beautiful wine country! The fruits of civilization! But the blood of peoples who had lived in Australia for fifty thousand years had been spilled all over that land.

It recalled the Crucifixion, as I thought about it—and the Eucharist—with bitter irony. The blood of the Aboriginal peoples that had been spilled on that land had been transubstantiated into the wine that conquering peoples and fellow-travelers drank to their own condemnation as they contemplated that beautiful countryside.

I had made every effort I could to acquaint myself with Aboriginal history and culture before my wife and I had left for Australia. But that effort, of course, had been piecemeal. After the conference, she and I had had only a few days to travel, during which we visited one of the great Aboriginal spiritual centers, the famous Uluru, a small, rounded red mountain with little vegetation, surrounded by vast and arid flatlands, in the center of the continent—thought of by some as the umbilical center of archaic Australia, the *axis mundi*. It was difficult, however, to separate indigenous meanings at Uluru from the overwhelming tourist ethos that blanketed, not to say suffocated, the place. As a result, I was at the edge of spiritual nausea more than once, even as I also was able to stand in awe of Uluru, now and again.

We took a tour to and around that holy mountain. A few miles from Uluru, we had breakfast in the dark of the early morning hours on a small hill. Before too long, we contemplated the sun rising and gradually illuminating Uluru at the horizon in front of us. Uluru emerged from the darkness as if it had been created from nothing. Then, with the dawn upon us, we proceeded in our bus to that ancient site itself. We walked here and there at its base, as our guide told us stories about Aboriginal life and art and history and spirituality. That tour-guide narrative sounded like standard tour-guide fare. But the experience of actually encountering Uluru, for me, was overwhelming. I picked up a hand-sized red stone from one of the parking lots. It was the same color as the smooth and sculpted walls of the mountain. Like an ancient pilgrim to the Holy Land, I brought that charged relic home with me.

Along the way, I pressed the guide with questions about water. The historic journeys of the Aboriginal peoples, he said, proceeded from waterhole to waterhole, especially in the parched regions of central Australia. At one point we went into what the guide called a cave, at the base of Uluru. It was, in fact, a huge stone shelf, extending like a porch over our heads. Inside, we saw some drawings on the stone in front of us, which the guide said were thousands of years old. I wanted to believe that. The most visible of those apparently ancient wall-drawings was a line of circles, each one executed as if it were the coil of a snake, an ancient Aboriginal symbol. The guide said that, in addition to their spiritual meanings, those images functioned to show Aboriginals where to find water holes.

The guide also told us another water story along the way, in response to my inquiries. The gigantic five-star resort where my wife and I were staying, not far from Uluru, was a huge consumer of water. I had wondered about that, since the resort had a large swimming pool and all the other "amenities" of most luxury hotels around the world. Each of the hotel rooms had a spa and two sinks, among other things. The resort also had a buried sprinkler system that watered its sizeable lawns every evening—right there in the middle of what for all intents and purposes was a desert! All the spacious rooms at the resort were, of course, air-conditioned. And I saw no signs of solar panels anywhere, to heat our shower water or to produce any of the electricity that the resort used so profusely. Nor did I see any signs that the resort's grey-water was being salvaged anywhere or that anyone had given any serious thought to treating the sewage that the resort produced, to reclaim at least some of that water.

Our guide told us at one point that the aquifer from which the resort draws its water is now thirty per cent depleted and that it is estimated that those precious waters will be totally depleted in another fifteen to twenty years. This, in a place where Aboriginals had survived and, in some measure, thrived, for tens of thousands of years! This situation made me think of a remark by Holden Caulfield, in *Catcher in the Rye*. As he was leaving the Radio City Music Hall Christmas Spectacular that featured scantily clad dancing girls, the Rockettes, in Manhattan, he observed: "Jesus would have puked." I was much relieved when we boarded our bus to the airport at Alice Springs. I had had enough of the tourist world at Uluru.

I felt more in touch with the dynamics between Aboriginals and Non-Aboriginals in church settings. There a painful conversation had been underway for some years. In this context, I found that the poignant book by the Australian Lutheran theologian Norman Habel, *Reconciliation: Searching for Australia's Soul*, was most helpful.[11] Habel reviews the poisoned history between the European settlers and the Aboriginals, with a focus on the often destructive role that the Church played, and then cautiously raises the question about moving toward some kind of reconciliation between Aboriginals and Non-Aboriginals.

Of interest to me was the way that Habel framed the conversation. With other Australian church people, Habel identified the Aboriginals with "the land" and the Non-Aboriginals—by default—with the ethos of the town or the city. Think Uluru, on the one hand, and Adelaide, on the other. Habel urgently wants the Non-Aboriginals who live in Adelaide to encounter the Aboriginal culture that once flourished at places like Uluru. Habel believes that the path to reconciliation between the indigenous and the non-indigenous cultures can be prepared in a number of ways, but above all by the development of a new spirituality of the land on the part of the Non-Aboriginals.

That may be true—in Australia. Contrast North America. In my homeland, historically, a "back to nature" movement on the part of non-native peoples, particularly the affluent who reside in or near cities, has been dysfunctional. The first chapter of my own theological reflections about nature began when I was wrestling precisely with this issue. In my 1970 book, *Brother Earth*, I identified a schizophrenia between Nature and Civilization in North America, which pitted one against the other.

That pathology is well illustrated by the two great American Henrys: Henry Thoreau and Henry Ford. Thoreau thought that Civilization—or "the city"—is dirty, artificial, and corrupt. Hence he fled to what he perceived to be the vital and purifying embrace of Nature. Ford thought that the promise of the human future was located in the midst of the machinations of Civilization. He cared little whether Nature was raped in the process.

In *Brother Earth*, I argued that a prophetic reading of biblical texts can show us a way to heal that American cultural schizophrenia: a way to give all, rich and poor, black and white, male and female, native and non-native, and all the other earth-creatures, too, the blessings of both Nature and Civilization, without desecrating either.[12] That kind of analysis, I am now very much aware, has whatever validity it might have only in an American context. The dynamics of the Australian cultural world, notwithstanding some parallels, appear to be quite different.

Be that as it may, in retrospect I stand convicted by the argument of my own book. Already when I wrote the *Brother Earth*, I was very much aware that I myself had been a victim or a perpetrator of the cultural schizophrenia that I had identified. In the years of my youthful innocence (as it were), I lived that schizophrenia. As a boy, I had a passion for Nature. I loved to visit Lake Erie and Niagara Falls. I loved to wander around the uncultivated fields and woodlots and the orchards near my exurban home. I loved to garden with my parents. Perhaps I was closest to them when we were working with the earth and harvesting its fruits.

I loved our family vacations, too. In those post-World War II days, we visited many of the nation's great national parks. On the other hand, those were the years of the Eisenhower presidency, the era of "Peace, Progress, and Prosperity." I was much concerned with politics at that time in my life. As the editor of my high school newspaper, I wrote editorials championing Eisenhower's causes, such as his launching of the great interstate highway system. I was a living example of that destructive cultural schizophrenia which I later diagnosed in *Brother Earth*, loving nature and loving the society that desecrated nature.

Fast forward to 2014, when I published *Before Nature: A Christian Spirituality*.[13] In that book I narrate some chapters from my own life story, how along the way I tried to respond to the claims of biblical prophecy in order to affirm both the rights of Nature and the rights of Civilization, particularly the rights of the poor of the earth, in a context where the forces of so-called Civilization are devastating the Earth and its inhabitants, to the point of no return. But I am not sure whether I have truly taken to heart the voice of biblical prophecy that I long ago identified. I am not sure whether or how much my own life has been healed. Maybe that's what was troubling me, most deeply, at Uluru.

I live comfortably with Nature, cultivated and wild, during most of the summer months. I live comfortably with Civilization, for better or for worse, during most of the winter months. But I have lived all the days of my life, whether in Nature or in Civilization, in a world of white privilege. I have always comfortably been a member of the white flock, as it were. I have studied and agonized about what it must be like to live outside that flock, to be dispersed among "the others," the black sheep, those excluded from the circles of the powerful.

I do realize that the blood of Native Americans was once spilled on the land of New England, reminiscent of the Australian experience—the very land where I scythe and garden and walk in the woods during the summer and where I sometimes seek to find a kind of refuge during the winter. I do realize that many of the members of the African-American inner-city church where I worship in Boston can easily call to mind the days of slavery and the culture of hangings (I recently took James Cone's book, *The Cross and the Lynching Tree*, off a shelf in my study and re-read it, cover to cover, a chilling experience[14]). But I do indeed live comfortably and in relative safety.

All of which is to say: whether I am in Australia or in the U.S., and even as I am now beyond my 80th birthday, my own contemplation of nature is still full of ambiguities and therefore still very much a work in progress. I love to behold nature, as Jesus commanded his followers to do, when he celebrated the lilies of the fields. But I am typically less eager to follow Jesus when he calls his disciples together in order to journey with him toward the Cross. I am not readily inclined to leave the world of my own creature comforts and my own theological securities, to follow Jesus into the wildernesses of America in order to encounter those whom my class generally considers to be the lost sheep and their world.

7

Bringing the Gothic Down to Earth

REDISCOVERING SAINT FRANCIS IN STONE

"So it is not the will of your Father in heaven
that one of these little ones should be lost."

(MATT 18:14)

Like countless intrepid souls, I have been fascinated with cathedrals for many years, but from what is probably an uncommon perspective: what they tell us about nature. I wrote about "The Gothic Spirit" in my 2008 book, *Ritualizing Nature*, whose cover showed one of John Constable's grand paintings of the Salisbury Cathedral.[15] My wife and I completed a fiftieth anniversary trip to France a few years ago, our first visit to that country. As a matter of course, we sauntered through a number of stellar cathedrals—and abbey churches—among them Mont St. Michel, Notre Dame de Paris, Chartres, St. Denis, and Rouen.

In preparation for this journey, I re-read a number of works from my own shelves, beginning with Henry Adam's celebrated *Mont St. Michel and Chartres*.[16] Having now encountered those two churches for the first time, I have decided that Adams tells us much more about himself in his book than about the buildings themselves. In striking contrast, George Duby's classic 1981 book, *The Age of the Cathedrals: Art and Society 980–1420*, takes us toward the heart of the matter, bringing the Gothic cathedrals down to earth.[17] Keeping St. Francis in mind helps us to do just that, and for good reason. The full meaning of Jesus' command to contemplate nature is at stake.

I had read Duby's book with some care in preparation for my 1985 study of historic Christian views of nature, *The Travail of Nature*.[18] But this re-reading in 2015 was much more exciting for me, since along the way I was able to immerse myself in some of the charged spaces that Duby discusses. Here I want to highlight his illuminating references to St. Francis (1181/82–1226), and then consider what I believe to be a more ominous character of the gothic cathedrals, spiritually speaking.

Consider these explorations to be a modest complement and an enthusiastic compliment for the still emerging theology of his holiness, Pope Francis, who thankfully has already, by his name, by his spirit, and by his encyclical *Laudato Si'*, done so much to revive the spirituality of the man from Assisi in our time.[19]

Duby shows how Catholic theology in the thirteenth century rehabilitated matter. It rejected both the pantheism of an Amaury of Bene ("pantheism" identifies the world with God) and the Gnosticism of the Albigensian movement ("Gnosticism" is the view that the spiritual alone, or God, is good, while matter is evil). St. Francis' rapture over the earthly creatures, says Duby, may well have been decisive in both these contexts. All creatures are, for St. Francis, *creatures*. They are not divine. Francis is not a pantheist. But, for St. Francis, they are also *sacral*, not something to be taken for granted, surely not something to be despised, as Gnostics have done throughout the ages. This kind of vision of a creaturely, but divinely charged material world, Duby explains, made reconciliation with the visible universe central to cathedral art.

Gone, then, were both the dark and conflicted view of nature sometimes given with the Romanesque and the strident anti-material sensibilities of the Gnostic Albigensians. Gone, too, were any pantheistic tendencies. Nature was nature, not God, for the great gothic designers and builders, even as nature was passionately affirmed and understood to be permeated by God. Thus, for example, as Duby notes, the transverse arches at Chartres "show God causing light and the stars to burst forth . . . , and [God] shaping the plants, animals, and, finally, [the human creature]. They in fact spread out an inventory of creation for the faithful to gaze upon . . . Henceforth the successive stages of creation of the world became a clear and lucid vision, a sight for all to contemplate."[20]

What was thus contemplated, Duby stresses, was the given world of nature, not Romanesque, sometimes monstrous, images of nature, nor any Gnostic degradations of nature. This meant that to engage nature "humans should look at and observe" rather than fantasize. "This new outlook made the fables, the fantastic beastiaries," says Duby, "all the figments of the imagination, retreat into the background."[21]

Post-Franciscan theologians, like Albertus Magnus (c. 1200–1280), reinforced these trends, Duby observes. Albertus wrote, for example, a *Compendium of Living Creatures*, "in which he methodically describes the features that characterize the fauna in the various regions of his native Germany." This shift, from the fantasized—and sometimes horrific—visions of the Romanesque era to the more empirical, but still mystical visions of the gothic world, is evident, Duby suggests, "in the shafts of the columns of Notre Dame in Paris . . . , [where] its effects become visible in the style of the plants that decorated the capitals."[22]

In the choir of Notre Dame, completed about 1170, Duby explains, this botanical decoration was still a purely mental projection expressed with geometrical regularity. "Ten years later," he observes, "when the first spans of the nave were built, the flora that adorned them was already closer to its living models; deliberate symmetry had vanished and the diversity of actual nature was visible, so that it is possible to identify a given leaf or distinguish a given species."[23] Thus "the ornamentation of a cathedral was not just a chain of samples. It was supposed to constitute, in itself, 'a compendium of living creatures,' a full and detailed inventory, the faithful reflection of a sublime coherence."[24]

I am grateful that Duby developed this reading of the gothic and nature so suggestively, with particular reference to St. Francis. Hence my theme: rediscovering St. Francis in stone. Look beyond, then, the countless statues of St. Francis in American gardens today, most of them recalling images of the saint preaching to the birds. Those statues, notwithstanding tendencies to sentimentalize, surely tell a certain truth, but by no means the whole truth.

Look rather at the great, historic cathedrals. Contemplate them through the lens of the spirituality and life of St. Francis. They display a captivating Franciscan story, for whomever has eyes to see. Viewing those cathedrals as St. Francis in stone brings them down to earth, which is critically important for the contemplation of nature today. St. Francis cared deeply about the little ones of this world, the godforsaken lepers, for example, or humanly scorned creatures of nature, like wolves and worms.

Read as St. Francis in stone, this is the message those cathedrals proclaim. The God of those magnificent structures is the God who loves every creature, not just us humans, and, more particularly, the God who loves every creature for itself, not merely as a blessing for us humans. For this God, every creature, however insignificant it may appear, has its own place and its own glory, in the greater scheme of things—especially the little ones.

This, too, as a matter of course, for Francis, is the very God who is known to us in *matter*, above all in the Creche and the Cross of Christ and in the bread and wine of the Eucharist, which of course are at the center of the cathedral experience. This is what those soaring cathedrals tell us, from altar to spires. A single gothic cathedral, much more revealing than a thousand garden statues, is St. Francis in stone. This is the Gothic cathedral brought down to earth, which brings a great spiritual promise to this, our age of ecological crisis. Matter matters.

But that, poignantly, is not the only way to read the testimony of the great cathedrals. It is possible to see them with other eyes: yes, they testify to the glories of the creation, but all the more so they testify to the heavenly destiny of angels and of humans who will be eternally saved. Read this way, the cathedrals point to a spiritual world above, and to the termination of the material creation, here below. According to this reading, the Franciscan love for all material things will be eternally abrogated. Call this the Gothic ascent to heaven.

Anyone who has ever as much as walked through one of those cathedrals will immediately recognize this architectural dynamic. Enter through the west door, and your heart will be carried aloft by the heavenly heights of the nave. Typically, the tall, narrow, and beautiful stained glass windows will command your attention by their verticality, as well as by their colors. Then as you make your way to the center of the cathedral that sensibility of being swept up into heavenly heights will be accented. Sometimes you'll be overwhelmed, especially when you stand in one of the many cathedrals that is organized around a great and all-transcending tower.

Today that is the image that first comes into view, too—even sometimes in our era of skyscrapers—as you approach a cathedral city. You see the elegant, all-defining tower. Sometimes, in the minds of some onlookers, both in the past and today, that vision of that Gothic ascent to heaven is the essence of the Gothic spirit. That, it turns out, was in fact the major theme for the earliest Gothic visionaries.

Consider the thought and influence of the fifth-century master metaphysician and mystic, Pseudo-Dionysius. Duby strikingly tells us about the grand coherence of the Gothic vision of nature's rich and vibrant complexities, with reference to Pseudo-Dionysius. Gothic art, says Duby, "embodied lucidity and respected the hierarchies decreed by Pseudo-Dionysius, establishing each and every element of the cosmos in its rightful place. This was an art that ordained an indivisible whole . . ."[25] What Duby does *not* tell us about, however, is the dark side of this vision of cosmic brilliance and coherence. That dark side, as I showed in *The Travail of Nature*, has to do with creation's eternal fulfilment, with the eschatology of nature.

The grand cosmic drama, for Pseudo-Dionysius, has two acts, the downward overflowing of the Divine goodness (creation), resulting in a resplendent hierarchy of being, adumbrated in both spiritual and material creatures, from angels, through humans, to birds, worms, and stones: then the return of all those creatures (salvation) to God above, but leaving the world of matter behind (except for resurrected human bodies). In this sense, for the vision of Dionysius, matter does *not* fully matter, ultimately.

This conclusion was given dramatic expression by the great Thomas Aquinas (1225–1274), whom Duby cites in his discussion, but not in this respect. St. Thomas took the vision of Pseudo-Dionysius for granted. This is the question. Will this grand and glorious world of nature, so brilliantly apparent in the universal Gothic vision, ultimately be saved? St. Thomas answers—No. The human creature, for St. Thomas, *will* be saved at the very end (or, at least, many humans), as will all the angelic creatures, but *not* the whole world of visible nature, apart from humans, the world so beloved by St. Francis. Ultimately, for St. Thomas, the great orchestra of all God's material creatures—except, again, for humans—will forever be silenced. The brilliance of the all-inclusive gothic vision will have been, in this respect, eternally extinguished.

Soberingly, this Dionysian vision was self-consciously celebrated by the very figure, who, more than anyone else, can be regarded as the founder of the gothic cathedrals, the statesman and the visionary designer of St. Denis, Abbot Suger (1081–1151). He was a champion of the hierarchical metaphysics of light, envisioned by Pseudo-Dionysius. Brilliant as it was, however, the vision that Suger claimed as his own let the material world to fall into nothingness at the very end, even as it celebrated the beauties of that world in creation and embodied those beauties gloriously in the cathedrals themselves. In this respect, the animating vision of Suger was laced with ambiguity.

This is the dark side of the great gothic cathedrals, which their theological champions have not always realized. The world of the birds and the worms and the wolves, of the water and the fire, which St. Francis so fervently loved, ultimately is to be extinguished. Only the human and angelic worlds are to be saved eternally. Which, of course, has the effect of devaluing, if not totally desecrating, most material creatures, particularly the little ones among them, the creatures whom many humans tend to ignore or even to trample on. Ultimately they are not worth saving, according to this way of thinking, even though they may have functioned to glorify God and to enable and to bless human life along the way.

This is why I found it necessary to keep St. Francis ardently in mind, whenever I stood in awe of those citadels of Divine grandeur, especially St. Denis, but also Notre Dame de Paris, Chartres, and Rouen. For, the man of Assisi never forsook the world of God's many splendored creatures in nature. He never aspired to ascend alone, or just with other humans, to heaven, along with the angels. For him, matter just didn't matter, it mattered eternally.

Hence he should best be remembered not only as the one who preached to the birds and calmed the wolf of Gubbio, but all the more so as the one who, toward the end of his life, dramatically included animals in the outdoor Christmas Eucharist he organized at Greccio, as a foretaste of the world to come, the Peaceable Kingdom. And more. According to his biographer, Thomas of Celano, as Francis was dying, he asked to be laid naked on the bare ground. There, at one with God's good earth, he kept singing his signature hymn, the Canticle of Creatures. St. Francis' life-long ministry was a celebration of the whole cosmos and all its creatures, especially his "sister earth, our mother." This was the only world he ever knew or aspired to know.

While it may make some spiritual sense, then, to remember St. Francis by placing sculptures of him preaching to the birds in our gardens, it is finally more important for us spiritually to celebrate his life sculpted in the stone of the great gothic cathedrals, as they can be seen to reflect the grandeur and the goodness of *all* God's creatures, both now and in the life to come—a promise which, thankfully, Pope Francis has now begun to hold up for the whole world to see.

8

Understanding the Contemplation

AN I–ENS RELATIONSHIP WITH NATURE

"Behold the lilies of the field, how they grow:
they neither toil nor spin, yet I tell you even Solomon in all his glory
was not arrayed like one of these."

(MATT 6:28B–29, AUTHOR'S TRANSLATION)

If we are commanded by Jesus to behold the lilies, as I believe we are, and if we are also under the influence of modern Christian theology, as more than a few Christians still are in these times, then we have a problem. Except for thinkers like Tillich, twentieth-century Christian theologians and their twenty-first century heirs, as a general rule, have not given much attention to the contemplation of nature.

The great Reformed theologian, Karl Barth, in the twentieth-century, is a case in point. Sometimes said to be the Protestant Thomas Aquinas, there are very few theological topics that Barth did not discuss substantively and brilliantly in his multi-volume *Church Dogmatics* and in his many other writings—except, that is, *nature*! Although he richly discusses God's bringing the world into being (creation) and God's care for the world (providence) in his *Church Dogmatics*, Barth states emphatically that theology has no business developing any substantive teaching about nature.

Perhaps more to the point, over the years it has astounded me that although Barth lived much of his life in Switzerland he never really wrote about the Alps! He once produced a long essay on the music of Mozart, for example, but never, in the thousands and thousands of pages in his writings, as far as I have been able to determine, did he produce any detailed discussion of those glorious Swiss mountains, certainly nothing like the ruminations of John Muir, the great American naturalist and Calvinist theological commentator, in his work *The Mountains of California*.[26]

I visited Barth once in Basel, as a young theological student. I had never been to Switzerland before. For me it was like some fabled peasant making a magical pilgrimage to stand before the great king in his mountain-top castle. But I came away from that visit thinking more about the Alps than about Barth. I also came away from that visit pondering what Barth had meant, when in response to the disclosure of my own dissertation topic—*nature* in Karl Barth's theology (!!)—he had warned me against any kind of interest in nature!

Now ordinary Christians, if I may call them that, are different, surely in North America. Many of them zealously look forward to Easter Sunday, for example, when their church sanctuaries are filled to the overflowing with lilies. On Easter Sunday, they then enthusiastically "behold the lilies." Some of these ordinary believers, like my own brother, also devote themselves to flower gardening with a kind of spiritual passion. And they rejoice in the beauty of whatever flowers they are able to grow. Some also travel to the seacoasts or to the mountains or to the great plains, where they find themselves standing in awe of nature in its larger aspects.

My own experience, in this respect, has been typical. After World War II, my parents packed me and my brother and sister into our station-wagon, along with a load of camping gear, and we set out to visit National Parks—I did not know then that the U.S. had many such parks thanks, in significant measure, to John Muir's passionate advocacy. Yosemite, Glacier, Bryce Canyon, Acadia, Crater Lake, Great Smokey Mountains, Grand Teton, Yellowstone, and others we visited over the course of several summers. For us, like countless other Americans, the contemplation of nature came, as it were, naturally.

So there's a disconnect between the kind of theology that Barth stood for and the experience of countless ordinary Christians, at least in North America. Can that gap be bridged? For the sake of those of us who wish to take Barth's critically important theology seriously, along with the contemplation of nature, this is a real problem, as I noted at the outset.

The challenge in this connection, I think, is "faith seeking understanding." Barth was deeply committed to this kind of theological enterprise, but he never chose to focus his attention, in any substantive way, on understanding the dynamics of beholding the lilies. This may be due, in part, to the assumptions he held about how humans relate to one another, on the one hand, and to all the other creatures of nature, on the other. *Barth took for granted that there are only two ways a human being can relate to another creature, either as a "Thou" or as an "It."*

I believe that, in fact, there are *three* kinds of relationships possible, the *I–Thou relation*, the *I–It relation*, and what I like to call the *I–Ens relation*. I want to explore these relationships now, in conversation with a great Jewish theologian, who was influential in Barth's time, Martin Buber. *I want to suggest that when you behold a lily, you are contemplating an Ens* (the Latin for "being").

In his small poetic book, *I and Thou*, Buber highlighted two ways to relate to others, the I–Thou relationship and the I–It relationship.[27] The I–Thou relationship, for Buber, is a relationship between persons, based especially on speaking. The "I" speaks with the "Thou," and so enters into communion with the "Thou." Communicating by speaking, in Buber's view, is of the essence of any I–Thou relationship. For the "I," the "Thou" is not an object to be manipulated, but an end in himself or herself, and embodied speaking is of the essence of that relationship. An example would be this: a human couple in love, expressing physical affection for each other. That relationship, in Buber's view, is not fully an I–Thou relationship until they speak their love for one another.

The I–It relationship, for Buber, is quite different. The I–It relationship characteristically means that the "I" enters into an objectifying relationship with the other, which thus becomes a object or an "It." A carpenter using a hammer is an example of an I–It relationship. Likewise for a natural scientist, say, dissecting an insect in order to study it or a medical student working on human cadaver. Notably, an I–It relationship is by no means necessarily negative. Think of a cardiologist repairing a defective artery. Think of humans clearing part of a forest, in order to establish their community.

The problem arises when an "I" relates to a "Thou" in an objectifying manner, essentially turning that "Thou" into an "It." Worse cases of this would be war or sexual exploitation, any kind of human-against-human violence. In such instances, the "Thou" is objectified. The person has become merely an "It."

Where does this kind of thinking leave us then when we try to make sense out of what it might mean for us to behold the lilies? Clearly the relationship to the lilies, as that relationship is presupposed by Jesus, is not an I–It relationship. You are not studying the lilies' cell structure or cutting them down, say, in order to plant a cash crop. You are contemplating them, not manipulating or otherwise using them. If when you behold the lilies, then, your relationship is not an I–It relationship, what is it? Is it an I–Thou relationship?

Not according to Buber. The reason? Reciprocal speech is of the essence of an I–Thou relationship, as Buber understands it. And while humans may speak to their plants or to their pets, those creatures do not respond in kind. Buber was, of course, not aware of experiments in our own time featuring humans, say, a Jane Goodall, speaking with animals. Nevertheless, he probably wouldn't have viewed that kind of communication as an I–Thou relationship, since, for him, an I–Thou relation entails full and intimate sharing, as in the case of friendships or marriage. For sure, according to Buber's way of thinking, a human who beholds the lilies of the field is *not* entering into an I–Thou relationship. In this case, there is no mutuality, no speaking one with the other. But, again, such a relationship is not an I–It relationship either. What are we to make of this?

Buber recognizes the problem here and in a postscript to the last edition of *I and Thou*, he addresses it. A certain kind of reciprocity in the relation between a human and a tree is conceivable, he suggests. The natural world generally is characterized by spontaneity. This is particularly true of the animal world, says Buber; with animals, we are at "the threshold of mutuality." But here there is no true mutuality, no constant sharing of inmost selves by conversing with one another. Buber grants, however, that he has not said the last word regarding this problem.

I think that Buber was on to something in his postscript. My suggestion is this, as I have already intimated: that we modify Buber's articulation of the I–Thou, I–It distinction, in order to speak of a third type of relationship, which can be called an I–Ens relationship. I want to describe such a relationship here. It is akin to the I–Thou relationship in many ways, but without speech.

The I–Ens relation is characterized by the existence of both terms of the relation in *a present moment*. Both poles of the relation have a certain fluidity, an openness to new possibilities. The Ens, in particular, is a present reality, not circumscribed by the detached inspection of the human eye. There is, in other words, a certain immediacy to the I–Ens relation. The objectifying mode of human consciousness does not come between a person and a lily of the field, as it does come between the two in an I–It relation.

The Ens, in particular, is characterized first by its *givenness*. An Ens does not fit into a utilitarian description of the world. Like a two-dimensional painting, it confronts me directly with an exclusive claim, a claim which will not allow me to pass beyond it, as it were, to set it in a larger schema of means and ends. I come to a halt and I contemplate that lily of the field. I do not immediately think about its cells or how, if I were to pick it, I might give it to a friend. As an Ens, that lily stands before me in its own right, a beautiful entity posited there for its own sake. I contemplate it and am captivated by it. I do not penetrate behind its sheer givenness.

Along with its givenness, the Ens also exhibits a certain *mysterious activity*. I cannot fully predict how the Ens will be from moment to moment. It will grow, decay, stand silently still, or disappear in a way which I cannot fully understand. The Ens also, in a variety of ways, has beauty, a characteristic which we instinctively understand, even though beauty is very difficult to define. Perhaps I could say this much. An Ens is beautiful, whether in a simple or a profound way—whether beautiful in a strict sense or sublime—because it is an integrated whole. It displays unity and diversity in harmony with each other.

These are some of the characteristics of the Ens, considered in itself. Among the characteristics of the subjective pole of the I–Ens relation, the "I," the mood of *wonder* is perhaps the most important. Wonder includes, first, a person's *total attention*. I have already referred to Luther's comment that if you would truly understand a grain of wheat, "you would die of wonder." Wonder includes, second, a person's *openness* to the Ens, his or her willingness to forget preconceptions of what the Ens is or should be. As John Muir once reported about a walk through a grove of tillandsia-draped oaks in the southern United States, "I gazed awestricken as one newly-arrived from another world."[28] That is to say, to enter into wonder, you must be predisposed to encounter the unexpected. You must put away the textbook or the guidebook and contemplate nature with your own eyes. Wonder also includes, third, the *willingness to become small and lowly*, the willingness to humble yourself, especially before things that are otherwise insignificant—the blade of grass, the piece of broken glass at the side of the road, the ant making its way across the picnic cloth. I must step back. I must know how to allot the Ens a space of its own. I must not automatically pass it by or manipulate it or kill it.

The mood of wonder is closely related to two others, *repulsion* on the one hand, delight on the other. The first is the mood appropriate for an Ens that comes from what the literature of romanticism sometimes calls the dark side of the world and what some American writers, more particularly, think of as the wilderness. The dark side of the world is symbolized best perhaps by Melville's white whale, Moby Dick. The whale comes from the ocean, "which is the dark side of this earth, and which is two-thirds of this earth."[29] With that whale in mind, one can say: "Though in many of its aspects this visible world seems formed in love, the invisible spheres were formed in fright."[30]

If wonder is sometimes and to varying degrees complemented by repulsion, at other times and also to varying degrees it is complemented by *delight*. One sees the Earth not so much as covered except for a third by the dark ocean, but being framed, in Calvin's words, as a "magnificent theater."[31] Hence, Calvin can say: "Let us not be ashamed to take pious delight in the works of God open and manifest in this most beautiful theater."[32]

The mood of the subject which is perhaps most difficult to describe— we have already met this in the words of Melville and Calvin—might be called *the sense for the presence of God*. As Calvin writes: "We see, indeed, the world with our eyes, we tread the earth with our feet, we touch innumerable kinds of God's works with our hands, we inhale a sweet and pleasant fragrance from herbs and flowers, we enjoy boundless benefits, but in those very things of which we attain some knowledge, there dwells such an immensity of divine power, goodness, and wisdom, as absorbs all our senses."[33]

Perhaps the fundamental idea here can be summarized as follows. In encountering the Ens, I am captivated by the En's openness to the Depths (Tillich) which underlie and permeate its givenness, its mysterious activity, and its beauty. Muir once expressed this in his own characteristic way by saying of a group of California redwoods: "Every tree seemed religious and conscious of the presence of God."[34] Of an Alaskan glacier, he wrote likewise: "Every feature glowed with intention, reflecting the plans of God."[35]

With such understandings of what an I–Ens relationship can mean, we then may have arrived at a place where we can deeply *understand* Jesus' command to "Behold the lilies of the field," as if for the first time. In response to this way of thinking, *theologians* may want to adjust or even radically change their theologies. And *ordinary believers* will hopefully have discovered an illuminating way for them to think about their own experience of nature, particularly when they behold the lilies on Easter Sunday.

9

Encountering the Beast of the Night

BEYOND THE LILIES OF THE FIELD

"He was in the wilderness forty days, tempted by Satan;
and he was with the wild beasts."

(MARK 1:13)

If we behold the lilies, and the lilies only, we haven't really beheld them, at least according to biblical testimony. That would be like celebrating the Resurrection of Jesus on Easter, as some try to do, without having first experienced the woes of the Cross on Good Friday. Consider, then, the powers of death raging throughout the world of nature, in particular the beast of the night.

I was probably not the only ninth grader who was once asked to memorize the first stanza of the poem by William Blake, *The Tiger*:

Tiger, tiger, burning bright
In the forests of the night,
What immortal hand or eye
Could frame thy fearful symmetry?

Not too far from the lilies of the field, in the nearby hills, lurks the beast of the night, created by God.

The traditions of faith which have been handed down to us in the Bible take such a fearsome presence for granted. In Psalm 104, for example, we encounter a powerful witness to the goodness and the diversity and beauty of God's created world, a kind of grand poetic commentary on the creation narrative of Genesis 1. In the midst of that rich narrative of peaceful unfolding, however, we read this sobering testimony about God: "You make the darkness and it is night, when all the animals of the forest come creeping out. The young lions roar for their prey, seeking their food from God" (Ps 104:20–21).

The Book of Job also takes such stark realities for granted; indeed it even celebrates them. Again, the lion: "Can you hunt the prey for the lion, or satisfy the appetite of the young lions, when they crouch in their dens'" (Job 38:39–40). And the raven: "Who provides the raven its prey, when its young ones cry to God, and wander about for lack of food?" (Job 38:41). And, again, the hawk and the eagle: "Is it by your wisdom that the hawk soars, and spreads its wings toward the south? Is it at your command that the eagle mounts up and makes its nest on high? . . . From there it spies the prey; its eyes see it from far away. Its young ones suck up blood; and where the slain are, there it is" (Job 38:26–30).

What we sometimes routinely call "natural evil" biblical traditions sometimes lift up with no less vividness than the witness of Melville in *Moby-Dick*, which I have already cited. With the White Whale in mind, Melville comments: "Though in many of its visible aspects this world seems formed in love, the invisible spheres were formed in fright."

What are we to make of the beast in the night, even as we are eager to behold the lilies of the field? To answer this question, I think it is helpful to be aware of some findings of the natural sciences. Can such findings enrich the testimonies of faith? I think so, more often than not. But you have to work at it, tease out the meanings, to allow that process of enrichment to percolate.

We can do this fruitfully, I believe, by invoking the metaphor of *consonance* advocated by Lutheran theologian Ted Peters and his associates. This means: as you listen to the testimonies of the Scriptures, you also keep your ears open for voices in the sciences that might resonate with and even help you to explicate the meaning of those biblical testimonies. This promising process of listening for consonance sometimes begins, however, with an uneasy sense of conflict.

A case in point: human table fellowship and violence against, and among, animals. The book *How Cooking Made Us Human*, by the biological anthropologist, Richard Wrangham, caused a stir in some scientific circles when it was first published.[36] Wrangham argued that 1.8 million years ago humans's use of fire to cook food made it possible for their brains to grow and for their digestive tracts to shrink, giving rise to our evolutionary ancestor, *Homo erectus*. Humans were freed from spending half the day chewing, like other primates, and could do other more productive things, above all using their brains to build and sustain a new kind of complex community life.

In all this, meat eating—violence against animals—was taken for granted. An earlier hominid, according to Wrangham, *Homo habilis,* had already adopted that practice a half million years before. In this sense, our Thanksgiving Day turkey festivals, predicated on the killing of animals and cooking their meat *and* on the time *we* have to converse with one another, is the kind of thing that makes us the *Homo sapiens* we are, for better or for worse, according to this particular scientific perspective.

Contrast the picture of Adam and Eve in the Garden that Luther gives us in his Genesis commentary. At one point, Luther imagines that Adam and Eve enjoyed *a common table* together with the animals. Here Luther is simply giving a vivid voice to the text itself (Gen 1:29–30), which clearly assumes that "before the Fall" Adam and Eve were vegetarians!

Contrast also the picture of Jesus with the wild beasts suggested by the Gospel of Mark (1:1–3). Traditional interpretation of this text assumed that Jesus' encounter with the wild beasts is part of *the temptation* he was driven out to face and to overcome, according to the detailed narrative that we have in the Gospel of Matthew (4:1–11). Recent study has shown, however, that this Markan text in all likelihood is intended to tell us something positive: that Jesus was a New Adam, living peacefully with all the animals in a new Garden of Eden. This image is of course also related to the vision of Isaiah: the promise of God is for a new creation, in which the lamb lies down with the lion in a Peaceable Kingdom (Isa 11:1–9).

It would seem, then, that "science" tells us one thing and that "religion"—evidenced by the witness of a Luther or a Gospel writer, Mark, informed by the prophet Isaiah—tells us another, and that they conflict! Is this, then, just another example of the popularly celebrated "clash" between science and religion? On the one hand, we have a vision of what is essentially human emerging in the practice of *violence* directed to animals (and sometimes rapacious cultivation of the land, too). On the other hand, we have a vision of what is essentially human created by God, originally, or redeemed, in the history of salvation, in a state of nonviolence.

The temptation for believers, faced with such an apparent conflict, is to by-pass the science and to fudge the violence by moving as quickly as possible to the story of the Fall of *humans*, in response to which the Gospel of grace can then be celebrated. But such forgetting and such fudging, should they happen, would be unfortunate, because that forecloses discovery of the enrichment that the findings of science can sometimes offer.

To this end, of course, we need to put our brains to good use, above all theologically. Many biblical interpreters read the Genesis stories of creation *one-dimensionally*, in a simple sequential time-frame, as a series of episodes, first a narrative of God creating the world and the Garden, in particular, then the Fall of humanity, and finally the history of redemption. But the Genesis creation texts can also be read, and suggestively so, I believe, *multi-dimensionally*.

It is possible to read the Garden story, for example, not only as a story of human origins, but also of *a Divine work in progress*. We can read it as the account of a human beginning, in other words, but all the more so as the announcement of what God intends to be doing as the narrative unfolds: not just as a story of a human "state of integrity" *(status integritatis)*, to use the traditional language, but also as an announcement of a pattern of Divine activity (*modus operandi*).

The second century theologian, Irenaeus of Lyon, thought of creation this way. He imagined Adam and Eve before the Fall, and indeed the whole good cosmos, were created by God *to grow*. The world was created good, in this perspective, not perfect. In this way the Genesis creation narratives can be read as announcing the beginning of the unfolding plan or the intention of the Creator for a history with the whole creation, to lead that good creation toward its eternal perfection. Irenaeus accordingly imagined the good creation as being set in motion and thenceforth governed by God so that it could in due course be transfigured in glory, when the day of the New Heavens and the New Earth, the Peaceable Kingdom announced by the prophets, would arrive.

This kind of theological envisioning of creation history as a work in progress then allows us to imagine a certain kind of "natural violence" *in the good creation* from the very beginning, in conjunction with the Creator's intention to work to establish a world of peace eventually. Biological death, in this sense, is part of the good creation. All creatures are created mortal. We can even find room in this Irenaean interpretation of Genesis for the evolutionary image of "nature red in tooth and claw" (Tennyson): because death is never an abstraction. It is always painfully real, sometimes excruciatingly bloody.

Note, however: this accent on the mortality of all creatures and the pain and suffering that is essentially given with the reality of death in the good creation isn't an imposition of some alien, non-biblical idea. On the contrary, the Bible itself knows about this kind of encounter with the world of nature as a world of violence. As we have seen, the Psalmist imagined the lions "roaring" for their prey, "seeking their food from God" (Ps 104:21). Job celebrated the sometimes blood-curdling alienness and the magnificence of the wild beasts (see chapters 38–40). The heirs of Noah, that great caretaker of creation, the protector of the species, who contemplated the rainbow promise of cosmic peace, were given permission by God to eat meat, judiciously and respectfully, to be sure (Gen 9:1–5), but to kill animals for food nevertheless. Something of this kind of vision of the blood-spilling wildness of nature more generally is probably also reflected in the Apostle Paul's classic witness to the whole creation "groaning in travail" (Rom 8:22–23, KJV).

Would we have noticed such texts and would we then have been eager to assess their import, had we not been listening also to the voices of scientists like Richard Wrangham? Possibly not. Examples of this kind of consonance of biblical testimony with the findings of the natural sciences, could be multiplied.

But this biblical and theological engagement with violence in nature is not the whole story, of course. For believers, as Luther taught us, the Scriptures are the cradle of Christ. And Christ was sent by God, according to biblical testimony, as the Prince of Peace (Isa 9:6), who is to usher in the end days when "the wolf shall live with the lamb" (Isa 11:6), and the violence of death will be no more (Isa 25:7).

Such a construal of the vision of faith thus begins with the reality of violence against and among animals, on the one hand, and with the presupposition, on the other hand, that the ultimate purpose of God, who is working from the very the beginning and throughout the whole sweep of creation history, is to bring into being a Peaceable Kingdom for all things, with Jesus viewed as the one who inaugurates that new Kingdom, once and for all, precisely the image suggested by Mark's picture of him—according to the most recent interpretation—being with the wild beasts. This multi-dimensional vision of faith—violence in the good creation in conjunction with the ongoing work of the Creator for peace on Earth—then ends with the narrative of the eternal triumph of God's Peaceable Kingdom, when all violence in nature will have been forever overcome. But there is more to this story.

Human sin disrupts that Divine history with creation enormously, of course, beginning with the first emergence of human life as we know it, presumably in the hearts and with the deeds of the first *Homo sapiens*. Of the destructive powers of human sin, biblical witnesses have been well aware, from the fratricide of Cain to the thousands of crucifixions wrought by Caesar and his legions. Called forth by God at some obscure point in evolutionary history to be a different kind of animal, a peace-loving animal, *Homo sapiens* became by that particular Divine calling an embodied spiritual creation, whom we may call *Homo religiosus*. But then a fateful change occurred, all over the globe, wherever humans found themselves: *in practice* they passionately and pervasively rejected that God-given calling for them to live a life of peace with God and with every creature.

We humans, who were and are brought into being according to the image of the self-giving God in the midst of evolutionary history, chose a way of life—and continue to choose—that in fact was—and is—self-aggrandizing, not self-giving. In doing this, we consciously internalized and indeed *compulsively exacerbated* the patterns of violence inherent in the world of nature from the very beginning. The violence of nature, often pushed to "unnatural" extremes in human history, thus became our way of living (*modus vivendi*), which in fact was a way of death (*modus mortis*), pursued only for the sake of power over others.

With our historic falling—for the Fall is a historical unfolding—excessive violence thus became the way of life—or the way of death—we regularly chose: against God, against one another, and against virtually every other earthly creature of nature, including the soil on which we walk.

In this way, people of faith can learn from evolutionary science about the sometimes alienating ways of God in the good creation and its history with God. In this sense, people of faith can learn that the ways of God are sometimes dramatically not our ways (all the more so in calamitous events like the tsunamis), as they stand in awe before the mysteries of God's sometimes violent creativity in the world of nature, from alpha to omega.

From the very beginning, in other words, God saw the violence of nature and it was good.

From the time of the emergence of *Homo religiosus*, however, God saw the excessive and compulsive violence wrought by human sin and judged it evil. And all along, God has been working—struggling, cajoling, persuading, inspiring, guiding, patiently enduring, even dying—to maximize peace in this world and to consummate peace in the world to come, through Jesus Christ, the Prince of Peace.

Such a vision of routine violence in nature generally and of exacerbated sinful violence in human history in particular, and the Divine remedy for every kind of violence revealed and established in the person and work of Christ, is, for me, exciting to contemplate. What the world needs now, desperately, is this kind of Gospel of global peace! And we can thank some voices of the sciences for helping us to uncover the specificity of that Gospel of peace, more clearly and more compellingly, it appears, than we otherwise might have been able to do.

That such explorations may well lead some believers to ask questions is to be expected: about humans' relationships with animals, especially. Doesn't the theological approach to creation-history we have considered here strongly suggest—even mandate—that Christians especially, we who are called to be peacemakers and a light to the world, should aim to be *vegetarians* or at least to *eschew violence against animals* whenever possible, following the example of St. Francis? Are we whom Jesus called friends not liberated by that friendship, in the spirit of Luther's image of our primal humanity, also to befriend our animal kin, to aspire in some metaphorical but profound sense to enjoy a common table with them in peace?

And then there are the lilies of the field. How are we indeed to behold them ecstatically, when we know that in this world the beast of the night is always lurking? Perhaps this is the best way to respond to that question. Wouldn't it be wise for those of us who do indeed want to contemplate the lilies of the field in this world of routine natural violence and excessive human violence, against both humans and the other creatures of nature, to behold these flowers in *a sacramental sense* as real signs of the New Creation yet to come?

Those lilies, in other words, are not just gorgeous flowers, although they are that, they also are a manifestation of the coming New Heavens and the New Earth, here and now. They are among the first signs of what the coming Eternal Spring will be like. They are embodiments of Eternal

Life, here and now. Perhaps North American Christians, if not other believers around the world, are wiser than they know when they gather lilies in abundance for their Easter Sunday celebrations.

10

Pondering the Darkness of Nature

THE NIGHT FLIGHT TO LISBON AND THE CROSS

"My God, my God, why have you forsaken me?"

(MATT 27:46)

"Father, into your hands I commend my spirit."

(LUKE 23:46)

I asked my wife to text my son this message: "We're about to board the night flight to Lisbon." "Cool," he immediately replied. He and I had watched the 1942 Humphrey Bogart and Ingrid Bergman film, *Casablanca*, many times. For that film, as all its devotees will immediately remember, the night flight to Lisbon was a central theme. Romantically but frenetically, *Casablanca* told the story of an escape from the powers of Darkness in North Africa, symbolized by the rule of the Nazis in those regions during the era of World War II. The night flight to safety in neutral Lisbon represented that escape.

Little did I know, however, as I boarded my own night flight over the Atlantic with my wife, for what I assumed would be a romantic adventure, from Lisbon to Porto in Portugal and then on to Santiago de Compostela in Spain, that this would also be a murky spiritual journey for me as well, a time for me to reflect about the Darkness of nature, with a fresh intensity. Not an escape from the Darkness, I hasten to add, but an encounter with the Darkness, as if for the first time. And then some visions of something far more real for me, the Cross of Jesus Christ.

We had booked a posh tour, if the truth be known. I was well aware of the ambiguities of such a choice. Popular essayists sometimes like to distinguish between touring and traveling. Touring is the quest for "interesting experiences," almost always presupposing five-star hotels, rich foods, and air-conditioned comforts at every stop. Traveling, in contrast, is the quest to explore unfamiliar lands and to encounter their contours and their peoples and their histories in a way that challenges, even overturns, the assumptions that the travelers carry with them. I would like to think that my wife and I were travelers in that sense, not tourists, even though our high-end cruise on the river Doro, which was the heart of our journey, had tourism written all over it.

Wishful thinking perhaps, but as we were guided around Lisbon, I soon realized that my inner self was preoccupied with strange things, dark things. The year 1755, above all. From the start, as our tour bus plied its way around the old city of Lisbon, I kept thinking about 1755, to which our guide had alluded, as he had asked us to notice the colorful, traditional tile-facades of the older buildings and told us about historical figures, men like Henry the Navigator, who had been memorialized in the form of large statues in some of the squares.

Portugal is famous both for its *azulejos*, the brightly glazed ceramic tiles first brought to its cities by the Moors in the sixteenth century, and, of course, for its so-called explorers. Not once, noticeably, did our guide refer to these heroes of the Western world as conquerors or colonialists or the like. But we did hear a good deal about all the gold they had brought back from Brazil and about how significant portions of that gold had been incorporated into the sanctuaries of the churches we visited.

But 1755? That was the year of Lisbon's catastrophic earthquake. "The scale of it is staggering," wrote a reviewer of Mark Molesky's study, *This Gulf of Fire: The Destruction of Lisbon, or Apocalypse in the Age of Science and Reason*.[37] And more: "Imagine the force of 32,000 Hiroshima bombs dispersed across 5.8 million square miles . . . It happened early on November 1, 1755, All Saints Day, when two plates a few hundred miles off the Portuguese coast collided, releasing a cataclysmic burst of energy that radiated in all directions." Lisbon was decimated. But that was only the beginning.

"Two other disasters befell the city in quick succession: a tsunami, triggered by the seismic event, carried thousands out to sea, and a devastating firestorm, fueled by vast reserves of debris, burned for days, killing thousands of the maimed and wounded who survived the quake, only to be consumed by flames and smoke."

In 1755, one of the great cities of the Western world at that time, a center not only of wealth and imperial power, but also of Catholic learning and piety, died a horrible death. The Biblioteca dos Reis, one of the foremost libraries of the world in that era, was destroyed, a loss that can be likened to the burning of the Ancient Library of Alexandria centuries before, according to Moleski. Many other venerable cultural treasures were lost as well.

But the toll in human suffering dwarfed every other effect of that colossal quake and its diluvial aftermath. Eighty-five per cent of Lisbon's buildings were destroyed. Some thirty to forty thousand of Lisbon's population of about 200,000 were killed. Those who remained after the initial rumbling had subsided were filled with dread. The reviewer wrote: "In the midst of such terrifying assaults on the senses—imploding buildings, heart-stopping noises, spreading fires, clouds of dust and smoke, the pitiful wails of men and beasts—a 'Wreck of Worlds' as one described it—many believed that Judgment Day had finally arrived."

I first learned the details about the Lisbon disaster in my studies of the history of theology as a graduate student. True, in 1710 the great German philosopher of the Enlightenment, Gottfried Leibnitz, had argued that ours is "the best of all possible worlds." In those times, confidence in Reason and Progress reigned supreme. After 1755, however, even champions of the Enlightenment such as Voltaire in France were driven to reconsider the most fundamental assumptions of their own era.

And, of course, with the wisdom of hindsight, *we* now can understand how spiritual despair subsequently could have come to command the minds and hearts of many in the West, as we now look back on 1755 from the perspective of the colossal destructivity of World Wars I and II and the Holocaust and Hiroshima and Nagasaki and the Indonesian Tsunami, among other momentous natural and human disasters since 1755. In such a world, well aware of calamities like the Lisbon earthquake, why not believe, with Friedrich Nietzsche at the end of the nineteenth century, that "God is dead"?

I imagine that no one on our tour bus, with the possible exception of my wife, had any idea about what was going through the mind and heart of this mild-mannered octogenarian tourist, who was stroking his grey side-burns and placidly staring out the bus window, as our group was introduced to the sites and the tastes and the churches and the shops of contemporary Lisbon. Be that as it may, it soon would be time to head north toward the city of Porto and the river Douro.

It had been raining heavily in northern Portugal before we arrived. So it came as no surprise to hear that our luxury river vessel had been ordered to remain at its dock. The flooding river was too dangerous for such a ship, especially near the several dams and their locks. That was a disappoint-ment, of course, but I secretly welcomed that news. I would curl up in my chair in the lounge with some coffee, and continue to read one of the two thick books I had brought with me, the first of which had kept me awake during most of that night flight to Lisbon.

That book was a traveler's delight, particularly in that land. Alas, I had never even heard the name of the great Portuguese novelist, winner of a Nobel Prize for literature, Jose Saramago (1922–2010), until I began to think about our trip. I decided to read what is said to be his most famous novel, *Baltasar and Blimunda*.[38] It was a charged experience, especially since I read it in its native setting. No reputable literary critic, I'm sure, would let me get away with the following utterance, but for me, in the privacy of my own soul, *Baltasar and Blimunda* resonated with the realistic anguish of Rolvag's *Giants in the Earth* and with the picaresque realism of Cervantes' *Don Quixote*. Whether one would also want to call it magical realism, I'm not sure, although the story is surely magical in its own way.

Saramago gives testimony to the Darkness of this world, sometimes subtly, sometimes with blood dripping from every sentence. His story unfolds in 1711, long before the Lisbon earthquake, but it's replete with human anguish and natural disasters all the same. The corruptions of hu-man power are everywhere in evidence, too, in the governing classes as a matter of course, but also in the Church's hierarchy and its monasteries. The Inquisition plays an egregiously dysfunctional role. Meanwhile the under-classes are everywhere put upon, not only by those in power but also by the contingencies of weather and disease, such as recurrent food shortages or outbursts of the plague.

Now and again, Saramago sharply tells us, the whole citizenry is entertained, as it were, when those identified as sorcerers or heretics or other enemies of the King or the Inquisition are burned alive. On one such occasion, says Saramago, as those about to be burned processed through the streets in chains and were being beaten by the whips of the guardian soldiers, the crowds were ecstatic: "They [wanted] to hear the whips crack and see the blood flow as it flowed from the Divine Savior."

Is there any Light in all this Darkness? Somehow, as Saramago's narrative unfolds, the visceral intensity of the human project does appear to have its luminous moments. His description, for example, of the labors of some of the fifty thousand workers struggling to build a new monastic church at the Convent of Mafra and of hundreds of oxen moving a colossal piece of cut stone up and over and down a mountainous road so that it could become the centerpiece of the west facade of that new church is riveting and suggests some sense of transcendental meaning. Notwithstanding numerous untoward deaths along the way, accidents of history, life seems victorious in such rare moments.

But the brightest luminescence in the narrative is what we see reflected, or refracted, in the compelling story of Baltasar and Blimunda themselves. A common soldier, Baltasar returns from combat missing his right hand. He finds a blacksmith who fashions him a hook—and, for other circumstances, a spike—to replace his missing hand. Baltasar then obtains some leather in order to hold each instrument in place, as needed.

Wounded, yet not without hope, he then happens to stand next to Blimunda in a crowd. She is a woman of deep intensity, whom the author describes as clairvoyant. There is no romance. In an instant they decide that they belong to each other. Then unfolds a relationship of intense loyalty, tender constancy, and passionate sensuality, notwithstanding the precariousness of their lives as unemployed members of the underclass in those perilous times.

Enter a learned and perhaps heterodox priest, Padre Bartolomeu, recently arrived from the Netherlands, where he had studied with the greatest scientific scholars of that era. He has a dream of building a flying machine. So, with the clandestine support of the King—the priest thereby has access to the financial wherewithal to allow him to construct his flying machine—he lays plans for what in his eyes is this scientific project. Again with the help of the King, the priest finds a secluded location where his flying machine can be secretly constructed. To that end, Padre Bartolomeu enlists Baltasar and Blimunda as collaborators. After many and extended labors, the three of them come to the point where they are ready to test-fly the machine.

Much to their amazement, the three passengers are lifted up into the air. They soar above the trees. Along the way, they fly over the site where the great monastic church is being constructed. The thousands working on that project witness that overflight and take it as a sign from heaven, announcing Divine approval for the construction of that new church.

After the tale of that overflight ends, Saramago's narrative is mainly one of decline, disruption, and sadness, befitting the historical dynamics of those times. But in the struggles of the people to construct the church, and all the more so in the authenticity of the relationship between Baltasar and Blimunda, and above all in the idiosyncratic inspiration of Padre Bartolomeu, we see that Light has shined, at least here and there, in a world of overwhelming Darkness.

If *Baltasar and Blimunda* is a stark, but in some ways hopeful, narrative of magical realism, the other thick book I brought along was, for me, a still more hopeful narrative of *believing realism*. I learned the latter construct from Tillich, who, in an era of cultural crisis in the early twentieth-century West, announced by German expressionism in the arts and by the French existentialism of Jean Paul Sartre and Albert Camus in philosophy and literature, sought to forge a new way to articulate the claims of the Christian faith.

It may sound strange to some, but my passion for good theology knows no end. Why not read a nearly seven-hundred page theological tome during a luxury cruise up the Douro? *The Crucifixion: Understanding the Death of Jesus Christ*, by Episcopal theologian Fleming Rutledge, turned out to be a well written and most insightful study, as a matter of fact.[39] I had chosen to read it by a deep personal necessity.

I had been trying to make sense out of the Cross of Christ my whole adult life. Why not try one more time, in this improbable setting in these my later years? What, in particular, could Jesus possibly have meant when he said from the Cross, according to Matthew, "My God, my God, why have you forsaken me?" (Matt 27:46) and, according to Luke, "Father, into your hands I commend my spirit?"(Luke 23:46) What, still more particularly, do these utterances say about the Darkness of my own soul and, all the more so, about the Darkness of our world? Do they speak hope in some manner? Can the Darkness of the Cross be encountered in any way as Light?

Fleming Rutledge published her *magnum opus* in 2015. A pastoral practitioner, rather than an academic theologian, she explored what is sometimes called the Atonement—the theology of the Cross of Christ—by intensely engaging the culture of *our* times, not unlike the existential approach of Tillich a century before. She also reviewed the history of Christian teaching about the Cross with fresh eyes.

In her view, the palpably offensive claims of some traditional Christian teachings about the Cross are no longer tenable. In particular, she rejects what is sometimes called the penal—for punishment—theory of the death of Christ. This is the proposal that the wrath of a harsh and judgmental heavenly Father had to be appeased by permitting his only Son to be killed, the Son being of infinite value. The idea was that "Christ died for our sins" by succumbing to the wrath of the Father which had been intended for us sinners. Some feminist theologians consider this view to be the sanctification of child abuse. The Father punishes and then kills the Son, according to this theology. Fleming concurs with the critics.

Still, Jesus *did* cry out from the Cross: "My God, my God, why have you forsaken me?" What are we to make of that cry of dereliction?

The death of Jesus Christ is undoubtedly the most difficult of all Christian faith-claims to understand. On the one hand, the Church has never sanctioned formulaic claims about how that Death is to be understood, as it did about the person of Christ or the Trinity. On the other hand, believers of all generations in the Christian West have attested that the Crucifixion is *the* single most important Christian affirmation of faith. This truth was illustrated in every church we visited in Portugal, where images of the Crucified and his wounds, statuesque or painted, abounded. I learned to take this truth with utmost spiritual seriousness when, as a graduate student, I first began my studies of Luther's theology, especially his "theology of the Cross."

I won't venture to summarize Rutledge's long and sometimes convoluted discussion here—it reads like a historical novel. But I do want to raise this question. What are the implications of Rutledge's discussion for the world of Portugal as portrayed in Saramago's *Baltasar and Blimunda* and as experienced in Lisbon in 1755? They are many, but I want to highlight only two here. For me, these utterances of my own heart, in response to Rutledge's discussions, are fragments of a believing realism. And they both have to do with the power of the Cross.

First, I believe that in Christ, God enters the world—God becomes incarnate in Jesus—in order to *bear with* all creatures that suffer, in ways that we mortals, however inspired we might be, cannot grasp. In that sense, no one who suffers is ultimately abandoned. In the Crucified, God Godself experiences the pain of our ostensibly godforsaken world and is present to sustain all suffering creatures in their pain: humans, animals, and perhaps plants (if they suffer).

This, emphatically, is in no measure intended to justify such suffering, of humans or of other creatures. That kind of theological project, I believe with Rutledge and with many other contemporary theologians, is *not possible*. But this is to say, as I have already intimated, that Jesus' words of dereliction on the Cross, "My God, my God, why have you forsaken me?," do not entirely express the meaning coming to expression at that moment.

Something of this extra meaning is captured by Luke's account of Jesus' words on the Cross: "Father, into your hands I commend my spirit." To me, this suggests that the Father did not forever abandon the Son, but was present with the Son in the Son's godforsakenness. And the Son embraced that presence, in trust, notwithstanding the Son's sense of absolute abandonment.

Likewise, for the presence of the Son, the Crucified, *with every creature* that suffers. God, in Christ, never abandons them. The godforsaken citizens of Lisbon in 1755. The godforsaken members of the underclasses throughout the ages, like the serfs who, in Seramago's narrative, arduously moved that huge stone along the mountain path, sometimes losing limbs or even lives, to help build that monastic church; and all the oxen, too, which were driven to exert themselves prodigiously and, sometimes, to do so beyond the limits of their physical strength, all along groaning as if in travail. Then there are the Jews and the gypsies and the heretics and the political prisoners in the story who routinely were whipped on their way to be burned at the stake. The Crucified, I believe, takes all such suffering on his shoulders and bears with them all.

Second, I believe that in Christ, God enters the world—God becomes incarnate in Jesus—in order to *inaugurate a new and eternal domain of Light triumphant, in order one day to overcome all the Darkness.* Fleming discusses this meaning of the Cross under the traditional rubric of Christ the Victor *(Christus Victor)*. The Scriptures envision this coming eternal era inaugurated by the crucified, victorious Christ, as a new creation, in which righteousness dwells (2 Pet 3:13), a time when the lamb will lie down with the lion (Isa 11:6).

On that Day, I believe, the godforsaken citizens who lived and died in Lisbon in 1755 will be called forth by God from the dead to inherit an eternal city of justice. Covenant partners like Balthsar and Bluminda will be reunited in a world even more beautiful than our image of the Garden of Eden. Heterdox believers like Padre Bartholomeu will be celebrated by all and will dance for joy—perhaps they even will fly like birds. Teams of oxen, which labored onerously throughout the centuries, often under human whips, will be reborn in eternal pastures, and, free of their yokes, will frolic like baby lambs. The crucified and victorious Christ will be the visible Good Shepherd of all creatures on that Day of eternal dawning, calling each one by name. His chief work in that eternal world of Light will be to serve as the Host for every celebration—and as the Celebrant for all who can understand him when he says of one sacred place on the new Earth: "Behold the lilies of the field."

Our river vessel finally got underway and made its way further up the Douro. The flooding had subsided. The next morning we woke up to see the little town of Barca d'Alva, the last Portuguese town on the river, where our vessel had docked. After a satisfying late breakfast on board, all climbed into two tour buses for a trip through the picturesque, vine-covered hills of that region, famous for their port wine. All but us.

My wife and I decided to absent ourselves from the tour, because we had seen enough medieval buildings in that region (one monastery had been transformed into a hotel; not an uplifting experience for me) and enough vineyards. Better sit in a chair, read, and contemplate the river. Maybe even snort a little port, before an afternoon nap. Modulate the effect of the grey clouds and the piercing rain, which had by then claimed the heavens all around us.

We both then withdrew to our own interiority in easy chairs where we could survey the river, lost in our reading and our contemplation.

Before too long, however, everything changed. The sun came out! That experience hadn't been in our plans! Forget the nap. Why not take a walk?

On shore, the first thing we noticed was the aroma of orange blossoms in the fresh spring air. We approached two orange trees in a field gone wild at the edge of the road. Apparently, they had not been cultivated for some time. But, for us, they could have been growing in the Garden of Eden. Their fragrance was heavenly and seemed to be beamed to us by the light of the sun.

Passing through the small village in quiet—its few stores were shut down for the day—we realized that it was Sunday. The Sabbath! We happened upon a muddy single-lane, two-track farm road that ran up a slight incline, taking us high above the river. It ran parallel to the Douro below and was dotted by a couple of small cottages, each with its own flower garden and orange trees. No one seemed to be around.

As we left the cottages behind, what did our wondering eyes behold? Rich banks of sun-drenched wildflowers on both sides of that muddy road, extending maybe a half mile. No lilies of the fields, but a profusion of gloriously colored blossoms: poppies, mallow, daisies, thistles, buttercups, wild roses, mustard, and others whose names we didn't know.

I am aware that in places such as Israel the picking of wildflowers is banned, and for good reason. But since ours was a solitary, single-lane farm road in a tiny town far, far from civilization, I gave myself permission to pick a few wildflowers for my wife. It so happened that that very day was her birthday, which I happily remembered just as I was about to give her that lovely bouquet. In my eyes, her face was then radiant as the sun and her smile was sweet as the orange blossoms. That moment, I later thought to myself, was a foretaste of the life to come.

Delighted with our walk, we made our way back to our river vessel, awaited the return of our fellow travelers, and began think about the last days of our journey: first a bus excursion to the university town of Salamanca in Spain, next down the Douro to Porto again, where we would disembark from our ship, and then ride a bus to Santiago de Compostela in Spain, the fabled destination of so many millions over the centuries.

At Santiago, with other pilgrims from many nations, some of whom had walked hundreds of miles, the two of us eagerly joined in the overflowing noon Mass in the Cathedral of this renowned city. "This is my Body"— *Hoc est corpus meum*—the officiating priest chanted. As my wife and I then stood jammed in line with people from many nations, pushing toward the altar, a holy crowd as I thought of them then, waiting to receive the Host, I began to contemplate the high, suspended, medieval sanctuary Cross above me all over again, and I was grateful.

11

Contemplating the Speaker

BEHOLD THE COSMIC CHRIST

"Who then is this, that even the wind and the sea obey him?"

(MARK 4:41)

A thought experiment. What if you were told, contrary to everything that you had ever been taught or otherwise had heard, that the biblical manuscript tradition that contains the text about the lilies of the field is totally corrupt? Under the aegis of such a supposition, you would have no reason to think that Jesus had ever said anything about the lilies of the field.

Next imagine this—an odious thought, but bear with me, for the sake of the important point I want to make: rather than Jesus, you would then be told, Adolph Hitler was the one who first said "Behold the lilies of the field." He *could* have said something like that. The Nazis had a theology of nature all of their own. Their propaganda about the Nordic race highlighted the sublimity, the vitality, and the raw powers of nature. Hitler, in particular, championed "the Teutonic" in nature, wolves and eagles, for example, but he was at times also given to sentimentality. Already in his twenties, he produced an undistinguished oil painting of red flowers in a vase (it was auctioned for $30,000 in 2015).

More generally, we know, as a fact, that in some of the concentration camps various Nazi overseers showed signs of what might be called cultural rot. Some listened to concerts that featured Mozart or Beethoven or Brahms, for example, even while the ovens of extinction were running. Anecdotal evidence suggests that several of the Nazi overlords at the camps also planted flower gardens or had them planted and cared for by prisoners. We can imagine that in some placid moments, Hitler himself might have been inclined to express tender feelings for beautiful flowers such as lilies.

Which is to suggest that while the command "Behold the lilies" has its own self-authenticating authenticity in *our* ears, accustomed as we are to hearing it in church circles or even in public settings, *the person who issues that command* will make an enormous difference in the lives and loves of those who choose to hear that command as meant for them.

This was assuredly true of the lives and loves of the faithful in the earliest Christian communities, which treasured and celebrated a variety of narratives about Jesus. The question that captivated their minds and hearts, perhaps more than any other, was the question Jesus had posed to Peter: "Who do you say that I am?" (Mark 8:29). Whatever Gospel traditions first century Christian communities held most dear—including Jesus' saying about the lilies—their experiences of *Jesus Himself*, the risen Lord, who had been crucified, was their core conviction. This is reflected by the fact, noticed often by biblical scholars, that the canonical Gospels, Matthew, Mark, Luke, and John, were "Passion stories with introductions." More than half of each Gospel is devoted to the Cross of Jesus, to events leading up to it, and to its aftermath. To adapt Tillich's language: for New Testament Christians, the identity of Jesus as the crucified and risen Lord was their generative ultimate concern.

This experiential centrality of Jesus, the crucified and risen Christ, in the lives of earliest Christian communities is dramatically expressed in the Gospel of Mark, our earliest Gospel. In response to the question from Jesus, already noted, "But who do you say that I am?," Peter answered him, "You are the Messiah" (Mark 8:29). This Petrine confession doubtless meant many things to members of the struggling first-century Markan community in Rome when they heard it. But among beliefs about Jesus they held most dear was this, the assumption that this Jesus, the Messiah, is *one with God.*

This is indicated by a text that appears early in Mark's Gospel: the story about Jesus calming the waters of the Sea of Galilee (Mark 4:35–41).

This is the narrative. The disciples and Jesus are on a boat in those waters when a "great storm" arises. The disciples are terrified. Jesus, who had been asleep, awakes. He then "rebuked the wind, and said to the sea, 'Peace! Be still!'" The waters then were calmed.

While the theme in the foreground of this story is the disciples' lack of faith, the background theme of the whole Gospel of Mark—"Who do you say that I am?"—is powerfully evident, too. The disciples in the boat, the text tells us, "were filled with great awe." And they said to one another: "Who then is this, that even the wind and the sea obey him?" (Mark 4:41). In a word: could this Jesus be the embodied presence of the Creator?

Members of the Markan community did not trouble themselves with questions about "what really happened" at the Sea of Galilee. That would be for later generations to think about, especially in the modern era. That *something extraordinary* did happen at the Sea of Galilee, that this Jesus the Messiah was indeed one with the God who sent him and revealed God in his powerful words and deeds, this they, or many of them, took for granted. But for the Markan community, the public answer to that question—who do you say that I am?—came only in the aftermath of the Crucifixion, the confession of the Roman centurion: "Truly this man was God's Son!" (Mark 15:39).

For that Markan community, then, this was the Gospel truth: the crucified Jesus was one with the Creator of all things. It would be reading too much into the theology of Mark's community, however, to say that, for them, Jesus was the "cosmic Christ." But whatever that expression may mean in our own time, it seems clear that the Markan community understood Jesus' words and works to be acts of the Creator God, who is attested in the Hebrew Scriptures.

We encounter a different, more pronounced accent on the same theme in the Gospel of John. The early Christian community that defined its faith in terms of the traditions that came to expression in the Fourth Gospel had a still more explicit vision of Jesus identified with the Creator God than the Markan community did. True, the Gospel of John was preoccupied with the story of the earthly Jesus, his signs and his ministry and his crucifixion as the manifestation of the light and the love and the truth and the life of God.

But for John, the ultimate horizons of this earthly Jesus were expressed much more vividly and much more consistently than in Mark. In John's Gospel, Jesus identifies himself with the Father: "I and the Father are one"(John 10:30). In John we meet, as well, an accent on Jesus as the cosmic Lord, as the agent of God in creating the whole world, using language that recalls the first words of the Book of Genesis, concerning God's creation of the world: "In the beginning was the Word, and the Word was with God, and the Word was God . . . All things came into being through him" (John 1:1–3). This is the very cosmic Word of God that "became flesh" in Jesus Christ "and lived among us" (John 1:14). Jesus, for John, too, is the One who comes from God and returns to God; and this God has placed "all things" (*panta*) into Jesus' hands (John 13:3).

Even more, other early Christian communities felt remarkably free not only to affirm, as the Gospel of John did, but, as it were, to revel in visions of the crucified and risen Jesus as the cosmic Christ. This is especially evident in the faith traditions that were most cherished in the Christian community of Colossae, a small town located in what is now eastern Turkey, about 100 miles inland from the great ancient coastal city of Ephesus. Small town or not, it apparently was the center of a thriving intellectual life that was rich in the traditions of ancient Greek philosophy, as those traditions had been reshaped and developed over a number of centuries: from Plato's *Timaeus* to the works of the Jewish philosopher and contemporary of Jesus, Philo of Alexandria, who had immersed himself in Greek culture.

So it happened that a number of intellectuals at Colossae projected a grand philosophical vision of the whole of reality, of all things (*ta panta*). This vision was vertical in character. It featured a variety of levels, with spiritual realities, such as angels, at the top and the visible material world toward the bottom, and with humanity positioned somewhere in the middle. For this worldview, too, the whole of that grand hierarchy of reality tended to be *identified with God*. In technical terms, the cosmic philosophy that was in favor in Colossae was pantheistic. The intellectuals of this school of thought in Colossae taught that all things are God and that God is all things. Theirs was an amazingly comprehensive vision of the world as God.

The writer of the Letter to the Colossians, the twelfth book of our New Testament—perhaps the Apostle Paul, perhaps a close associate of his— worked with the grand philosophical vision that was taken for granted by many intellectuals in Colossae, but radically revised it. He identified *Jesus and indeed the Cross of Jesus* as the all-defining central principle of the whole universe. He also took it for granted that the universe itself is *not* God ("pantheism"), but God's creation (a view sometimes called "theism"). In this sense, for the writer of Colossians—in vivid contrast to the vision of

William Butler Yeats in our era—the Center *can* hold. The Center *can* hold, because the Center is the Creator God in the person of Jesus Christ, crucified and risen, embracing and uniting all things in his person.

I'm aware that this kind of thinking about Christ as the Center of all things goes against the grain of the approach to the world which many people take for granted today. Call this popular way of thinking *generalistic*. It's an approach to our experience in this world which makes sense in a lot of ways—*common sense*. You identify a kind of coherence in the whole universe of your experience and you interpret individual events in terms of that worldview, not the other way around. If my wife of more than fifty years were to tell me what sounded like a disturbing untruth, I would not immediately call her a liar. I would think of the patterns of her entire life as I have known them, and try to figure out what she had meant in this particular instance. And, I'm sure, I would discover either that I had misunderstood her intended meaning or that she had not communicated her intended meaning clearly enough—or both. It would have been foolish indeed for me to make a judgment about my wife's character on the basis of a single, apparently exceptional event.

Another example. Natural scientists *must* be generalistic. They must interpret particular phenomena in terms of universal laws that are widely recognized within the scientific community. Many of us take that kind of scientific thinking for granted. If, for example, I think I saw a flying saucer, as a matter of course I would turn on the radio or go on line to see if anyone else had noticed such a phenomenon and, if so, what the meteorologists (I guess it might well be a weather phenomenon) are saying about the matter. I would not then and there reconstruct my whole understanding of the physical world, on the basis of such a single siting. I wouldn't be tempted to believe, for example, that interspatial aliens have been watching us and perhaps even readying themselves to engage us in some fashion. That's the common sense praxis of the natural sciences, akin to the common sense praxis of ordinary interpersonal experience. The particular is best judged in terms of the general.

Biblical thinking, in contrast, is typically, although not always, *particularistic*. For the Bible the most fundamental judgments about the whole of reality are to be made on the basis of singular events. This biblical way of seeing things is predicated on what might be called *fiducial sense*, not on common sense ("fiducial" from the Latin, meaning trust or faith). I once heard the Presbyterian theologian Paul Lehmann begin a discussion of this matter with this observation: "how odd of God to choose the Jews." According to the witness of the Christian scriptures, that is precisely what God did. God chose *one* nation from all the nations of the world—indeed a rather obscure and historically unimportant nation—to be a Light to *all* the nations. Then, according to the same scriptures, God further particularized God's saving purposes by choosing *a single person* from the Chosen People, Jesus, an obscure rabbi who gained his fame in the countryside not in the holy city, Jerusalem, to be the Light of *the whole world*. A leading Reformed theologian of the last century, Emil Brunner, called this kind of thinking "the scandal of particularity." Scandalous or not, this is the bedrock conviction of the Christian scriptures: in the life history of this particular rabbi, a son of the Chosen People, the ultimate meaning of all things (*ta panta* in the Greek) is finally disclosed. In this case, from the point of view of our fiducial sense, the particular reveals the transcendental meaning of the general.

So the witness of Colossians to Jesus Christ as the Center of all things may indeed sound odd to those who as a matter of course think about their experience only in terms of common sense, be it interpersonal or scientific. But for those who think also in terms of fiducial sense, that is, in terms of the witness of the faith that comes to expression in the scriptures, the scandal of particularity is, on its own terms, no scandal at all. From faith's angle of vision, that's just the way God has chosen to work God's purposes in this world. The particular reveals, for faith, what is ultimately going on in our universe.

This particularistic fiducial sense, it's important to note, does not abrogate our generalistic common sense. The confessions of faith have to do with *ultimate* things. The judgments of our minds have to do with *everyday* things. The ultimate is one thing, the penultimate another. Indeed the first comprehends the second and in that sense affirms it. In other words, these two kinds of knowing need not necessarily be in conflict with each other, although they may be, and sometimes are, in tension with one another. To say this much, however, is by no means to answer all or even most of the questions that arise when we consider how ultimate and penultimate things relate to each other. But it is to identify the particularistic kind of faith I'm talking about here, which, I believe, is taken for granted by many, if not all, biblical texts, and by the writer of the Letter to the Colossians, for sure.

Imagine this, then: the very Jesus whom we can envision beckoning us to behold the lilies of the field is now to be contemplated as the crucified and risen One, *who works like some unimaginably powerful cosmic mag-net, holding all things* (ta panta) *together and, indeed, in so holding, at once moving all things forward toward a universal consummation* when, as Paul announces, "God will be all in all" (see 1 Cor 15:28).

I want to share the summary statement of that vision, by the author himself, here. This is the best way, I think, to begin to grasp the all-inclusive, Cross-centered radicalness of the grand cosmic vision of The Letter to the Colossians. Maybe even read these words aloud. In their original setting, indeed, they appear to have been words of a hymn. They should best be read as if they're being sung: *"He is the image of the invisible God, the first-born of all creation, for in him all things* (ta panta) *were created, in heaven and on earth, visible and invisible, whether thrones or dominions or principalities or authorities—all things were created through him and for him. He is before all things, and in him all things hold together. He is the head of the body, the Church; he is the beginning, the first-born from the dead, that in everything he might be preeminent. For in him all the fullness of God was pleased to dwell, and through him to reconcile to himself all things, whether on earth or in heaven, making peace by the blood of his cross"* (Col 1:15–20).

I was taught as a child to sing "Beautiful Savior, King of Creation." We sang that hymn in Sunday School, words like these, with gusto: "Fair are the meadows, / Fair are the woodlands, / Robed in flow'rs of blooming spring; / Jesus is fairer, Jesus is purer, / He makes our sorrowing spirit sing."[40] That was good and pious singing: to envision Jesus the savior in the midst of the beauties of nature, here on God's good earth. But never was I taught anything in my early years like the amazing and nearly incomprehensible vision portrayed by the Letter to the Colossians! The Beautiful Savior I was taught to know and to love was, in fact, the Jesus portrayed in the Gospels, particularly the Jesus who taught us to behold the lilies of the field. In this respect, I was by no means atypical.

After the New Testament era, the teaching traditions of the Christian Church in the West focused more and more on the Jesus pictured in the Gospels, especially on the historical Crucifixion narrative, and less and less on the Jesus portrayed cosmically in the Letter to the Colossians. Indeed, as I have already noted, the canonical Gospels can be thought of as "Passion stories with introductions." They were stories of Jesus' way to the Cross, a pilgrimage of human fidelity that they described in rich detail. That trend became all the more dominant during the western Middle Ages, as anyone who has visited one or more of the great historic cathedrals in the West will have observed. Crucifixes displaying the body of the Savior, in the midst of or in the aftermath of the throes of suffering and death, are everywhere. Often, too, you encounter dramatic carvings or paintings depicting the "stations of the Cross."

But that kind of piety, and in many respects the theology that solidified that piety, envisioned the Crucified more and more as the savior *of humans,* chiefly if not exclusively, and less and less as the redeemer of the whole creation. By the end of the western Middle Ages and then on into the modern period in the West, indeed, the witness of the Letter to the Colossians to the savior *of the whole cosmos* had more or less been eclipsed.

This was nowhere more evident than in some major streams of modern North American Protestant piety, which focused mainly on the life of Jesus and his role as the believer's "personal Savior." Such trends were reflected dramatically in Protestant altar art of the era, where scenes from the life of Jesus, such as large images of Jesus as the tender Good Shepherd, tended to replace likewise large but wrenching images of the Crucified. These trends gained a kind of apotheosis in the twentieth century in the form of Warner Sallman's 1941 painting of the Head of Christ, which many Protestants in North America virtually idolized (it sold more than 500 million copies). The popular hymn that I loved so much as a child, Beautiful Savior, was an expression of those trends.

But that approach to interpreting the whole New Testament mainly in terms of the life-of-Jesus narrative and its meaning for the individual believer has recently begun to change, thankfully. Yes, the central traditional theological meanings of the life, death, and resurrection of Christ have continued to be emphasized, along with accents on the faith of individual believers. But the figure of the Crucified that is emerging in recent theological discussions now has taken on—again—cosmic proportions. And the vision of the Letter to the Colossians is at the center of these discussions.

This recent wave of theological interest in the cosmic Christ began to be visible for all to see in 1961 at the World Council of Churches' New Delhi Assembly. In a keynote address, a then not widely known American Lutheran theologian, Joseph Sittler, lifted up the dramatic cosmic vision of Colossians 1:15–20.[41] In his address, he prophetically called attention to the then increasingly visible degradation of nature all over the Earth. He also called upon the churches of the world to seek unity, not just in general, but specifically in the name of the cosmic Christ, who would be understood as the center of the whole universe and of all its nearly infinite temporal and spatial reaches.

Since 1961 many other theologians have raised their voices in behalf of similar themes. Thus in recent years there has been a revival of interest in the thought of the Catholic mystical visionary, the Jesuit theologian and paleontologist, Pierre Teilhard de Chardin, whose thought in the first half of the twentieth century had already been replete with explorations in cosmic Christology (alas, early in the same century, a number of Teilhard's works were banned by the Vatican).[42] The prominent German Reformed theologian, Jürgen Moltmann, acknowledging his debt to Sittler, has written suggestively about the cosmic mission of Jesus Christ, as well as about the earthly claim that the same Christ calls forth, for the sake of both ecological renewal and justice for the poor and the oppressed.[43] The influential American Catholic theologian Elizabeth Johnson has addressed similar issues regarding the cosmic vocation of Jesus Christ with compelling insight, especially in her study, *Ask the Beasts: Darwin and the God of Love*.[44] Others have also made significant contributions to the field of cosmic Christology. Most dramatically, perhaps, Pope Francis has made themes of the cosmic Christ his own in his celebrated 2015 encyclical, *Laudato Si': On Care for Our Common Home*.[45]

We should welcome all these developments, I believe, for two reasons. *First*, if we claim the Jesus of the lilies of the field alone as the Jesus whom we know best and whose story we want to share not just in our own circles but with friends anywhere who have expressed interest in Jesus, then we are *not* in a position to tie Jesus in substantially with the entire cosmos, as we know it today. The cosmos in which we live is quite different from the world familiar to the author of the Letter to Colossians. It is also quite different from the cosmos familiar to Augustine and Thomas Aquinas and to Luther and Calvin, even different from the cosmos known to the father of modern physics, Isaac Newton. The work of scientists such as Albert Einstein and his successors has bequeathed to us a radically new image of our cosmos.

Ours is an evolutionary cosmos of unimaginable immensity, not just evolutionary here on planet Earth, but universally evolutionary: from the era of the Big Bang 13 billion years ago, to our own time and on into a nearly infinite cosmic future. The number of *galaxies* in our universe, it has recently been calculated, is hundreds of billions. Remarkably, the all-comprehending vision of the Letter to the Colossians deals with such cosmic immensities (although that text's vision was tiny compared to that of contemporary cosmological physics), surely in ways that challenge comprehension, but at least in an all-inclusive manner—with Jesus and his Cross at the center of all things.

Second, if we claim the Jesus of the lilies of the field as the Jesus whom we know best and who's story we want to share not just within the household of faith, but with any friends anywhere who have expressed interest in the meaning of Jesus, then we are not in a position to address the global ecojustice crisis that has become *the* challenge of human history in these times. What's to stop an accent on beholding the lilies sounding like some escapist romanticism? What, on the face of it, does such a Jesus—the Beautiful Savior—have to do with polluted air or melting icebergs or the death of countless animal and plant species—including flowers?

But if we can find a way to live ourselves into the cosmic vision we encounter in the Letter to the Colossians, we may be able to find a way to narrate how Jesus, as the One in whom all things hold together, has already claimed not only the billions and billions of galaxies, but also the air and the icebergs and the animal and plant species of this Earth as his own, long before we humans ever came to understand how all these phenomena are interrelated, indeed from the very beginnings of cosmic history. Jesus the Beautiful Savior now can be celebrated also as Jesus the Universal Savior.

The Jesus whom the Church confesses, in other words, has a cosmic as well as a terrestrial reach. He is not just my personal Savior, by any means. Nor is he just the one who commands us to behold the lilies. I do confess, when God gives me occasion to do so, that Jesus *is* my personal Savior. And I am in love with the Jesus who commands me to behold the lilies of the field. Likewise, I have chosen to give my life to the Jesus who proclaimed liberation for the poor and the oppressed creatures of this world.

But I also worship the same Jesus, crucified and risen, who is the Divine Center of all things, in whom all things hold together, from beginning to ending, from before the Big Bang to the Consummation of the universe and who, more particularly, has claimed the whole Earth as his beloved ark, all its oceans and continents, all its mountains and plains and seacoasts, all its plants and animals, large and small, all its communities of human habitation, the cities and the farmlands and the wilderness regions. To use a term treasured by the ancient Church, the Jesus who is my personal Savior and who I believe is the liberator of the oppressed of this Earth is also the *Pantokrator*, the Lord of All Things. This is whom I see when I ponder the speaker who commands me to "Behold the lilies."

For Further Reading

AN ANNOTATED BIBLIOGRAPHY

Buxton, Graham, and Norman Habel, eds. *The Nature of Things: Rediscovering the Spiritual in God's Creation.* Eugene, OR: Pickwick Publications, 2016.

Papers from an international ecumenical colloquium that addressed some of today's most challenging ecological issues theologically, with instructive commentaries by the editors.

Chase, Steven. *Nature as Spiritual Practice.* Grand Rapids: Eerdmans, 2011.

A study of how nature can be a companion and guide for those who are invested in Christian spirituality.

Dahill, Lisa E., and Martin-Schramm, James B., eds. *Eco-Reformation: Grace and Hope for a Planet in Peril.* Eugene, OR: Cascade Books, 2016.

Rich discussions of the Reformation tradition's theological promise for a world in ecological crisis, on the occasion of the Reformation's five-hundredth anniversary.

Francis, Pope. *Laudato Si': Caring for our Common Home.* Brooklyn: Melville House, 2015.

Perhaps the single most important Christian statement in ecological theology and spirituality and ecojustice ethics in our time.

Horrell, David. G., et al., eds., *Ecological Hermeneutics: Biblical, Historical, and Theological Perspectives*. London: T. & T. Clark, 2010.

An excellent collection of short studies of Christianity and ecological issues throughout the ages, written in accessible form by reputable scholars.

Johnson, Elizabeth A. *Ask the Beasts: Darwin and the God of Love*. London: Bloomsbury, 2014.

Already a classic in Catholic reflection about evolution, faith, ethics, and spirituality.

———. *Consider Jesus: Waves of Renewal in Christology*. New York: Crossroads, 1990.

An accessible, but deeply thoughtful statement about Jesus, viewed in the context of our multicultural, pluralistic, and ecologically global world.

Moe-Lobeda, Cynthia. *Resisting Structural Evil: Love as Ecological-Economic Vocation*. Minneapolis: Fortress, 2013.

Suggestively views ecological issues against the background of concrete and complex social and economic trends, and proposes a classical, but reformulated Christian response—an ethic of love.

Moltmann, Jürgen. *God in Creation: A New Theology of Creation and the Spirit of God*. Translated by Margaret Kohl. San Francisco: Harper & Row, 1984.

A landmark publication by one of the leading theologians of our era, with a thoroughgoing affirmation of the whole creation as the milieu of God's presence and purpose to redeem all things, concretely focusing on the works of the Spirit.

Nash, James A. *Loving Nature: Ecological Integrity and Christian Responsibility*. Nashville: Abingdon, 1991.

An early classic in Christian ecological ethics, which still merits careful attention.

Peters, Ted, *God—The World's Future: Systematic Theology for a Postmodern Era*. Minneapolis: Fortress, 1992.

A well-written, comprehensive statement of the meaning of the Christian faith for the whole creation in these times of spiritual, cultural, and global crisis.

Rasmussen, Larry. *Earth Community, Earth Ethics*. Maryknoll, NY: Orbis, 1996.

An award-winning study of how a global religious ethic can speak to many audiences in our time and also inspire individual believers and religious communities to meaningful political action.

Rossing, Barbara, *The Rapture Exposed: the Message of Hope in the Book of Revelation*. Boulder, CO: Westview, 2004.

An insightful study of the book of Revelation that shows that biblical hope is focused on a new heavens and a new earth for all creatures, not the "rapturing up to heaven" of a few, select humans.

Santmire, H. Paul, *Before Nature: A Christian Spirituality*. Minneapolis: Fortress, 2014.

Invites the reader to join in a theological and spiritual journey to a contemplative knowledge of the triune God through a deep relationship with the cosmic and universal ministry of Christ and the Spirit.

———. *Brother Earth: Nature, God, and Ecology*. New York: Nelson, 1970.

A programmatic statement in ecological theology in its earliest years.

———. *Nature Reborn: The Ecological and Cosmic Promise of Christian Theology*. Minneapolis: Fortress Press, 2000.

A brief introduction to ecological theology at the turn of the century.

———. *Ritualizing Nature: Renewing Christian Liturgy in a Time of Crisis*. Minneapolis: Fortress 2008.

Argues that Christian liturgy is the Church's mode of identity-formation and that therefore an ecological approach to Christian worship is critically important in these times of global crisis.

———. *The Travail of Nature: The Ambiguous Ecological Promise of Christian Theology.* Minneapolis: Fortress, 1985.

A review of historic Christian attitudes to nature, identifying two streams in Christian theology over the centuries, the "spiritual" and the "ecological," showing that while historic Christian thought is sometimes ecologically problematic, it is also at other times ecologically rich, insightful, and promising.

Sittler, Joseph. *Evocations of Grace: Writings on Ecology, Theology and Ethics.* Edited by Peter Bakken and Steven Bouma-Prediger. Grand Rapids: Eerdmans, 2000.

Selected works by one of the great ecotheologians of the twentieth-century, with instructive interpretation by the editors.

Southgate, Christopher. *The Groaning of Creation: God, Evolution, and the Problem of Evil.* Louisville: Westminster John Knox, 2008.

Perhaps the best single book about the—unsolvable?—theological problem of evil in nature.

Tillich, Paul. "Nature and Sacrament." In *The Protestant Era*, 94–114. Translated by James Luther Adams. Chicago: University of Chicago Press, 1957.

A short but compelling essay—a "classic"—by one of the leading theologians of our era identifying the historical rationale for fresh and deep attention to the theology of nature in a world which in many respects is structurally and spiritually antinature.

Author's Note

Readers of my other writings will meet a few familiar sketches, reflections, and reminiscences in this primer. For me, these extant discussions, revised and adapted here, take on new significance in this setting: fresh growth, as it were, from well-turned soil. I hope that readers of this book who know my other writings will engage these older thoughts in that new spirit.

These are the discussions that may be familiar to you: **1**, Scything With God (in part from *Before Nature*, 2014); **3**, Taking a Plunge in the Niagara River (in part from *Before Nature*, 2014); **4**, Walking Along the Charles River (in part from *Ritualizing Nature*, 2008); **7**, Bringing the Gothic Down to Earth (in part from *Dialog*, 55/1 [2016] 9–12); and **8**, Understanding the Contemplation (in part from the *Journal of Religion* 48/3 [1968] 260–73).

Endnotes

1 Pope Francis, *Laudato Si': Caring for Our Common Home* (Brooklyn: Melville House, 2015).

2 H. Paul Santmire, *Brother Earth: Nature, God, and Ecology in a Time of Crisis* (New York: Nelson, 1970); Santmire, *Before Nature: A Christian Spirituality* (Minneapolis: Fortress, 2014).

3 Joseph Sittler, *Evocations of Grace: The Writings of Joseph Sittler on Ecology, Theology, and Ethics*, ed. Steven Bouma-Prediger and Peter Bakken (Grand Rapids: Eerdmans, 2000), 80.

4 Søren Kierkegaard, *What We Learn from the Lilies of the Field and the Birds of the Air* (Minneapolis: Augsburg, 1948), 203-4.

5 Katherine Hart, *Eric Aho Ice Cuts* (Hanover, NH: Hood Museum of Art, Dartmouth College, 2016), 4.

6 Ibid., 9.

7 David Gagne, St. Paul, Minnesota; private conversation, May 10, 2015.

8 Lisa E. Dahill, "Into Local Waters: Rewilding the Study of Christian Spirituality," *Spiritus: A Journal of Christian Spirituality* 16 (2016) 141–165.

9 Dietrich Bonhoeffer, *The Cost of Discipleship*, trans. Reginald H. Fuller (New York: Simon & Schuster, 1995).

10 The papers from this consortium have now been published: *The Nature of Things: Rediscovering the Spiritual in God's Creation*, ed. Graham Buxton and Norman Habel (Eugene, OR: Pickwick Publications, 2016).

11 Norman Habel, *Reconciliation: Searching for Australia's Soul* (Eugene, OR: Wipf & Stock, 1999).

12 See note 2 above.

13 See note 2 above.

14 James H. Cone, *The Cross and the Lynching Tree* (Maryknoll, New York: Orbis Books, 2011).

15 H. Paul Santmire, *Ritualizing Nature: Renewing Christian Liturgy in a Time of Crisis* (Minneapolis: Fortress, 2008).

16 Henry Adams, *Mont-Saint-Michel and Chartres* (New York: Penguin Classics, 1986).

17 George Duby, *The Age of the Cathedrals: Art and Society, 980–1420*, tr. Eleanor Levieux and Barbara Thompson (Chicago: University of Chicago Press, 1981).

18 H. Paul Santmire, *The Travail of Nature: the Ambiguous Ecological Promise of Christian Theology* (Minneapolis: Fortress, 1985).

19 Pope Francis, *Laudato Si'*.

20 Duby, *The Age of the Cathedrals,* 115.

21 Ibid., 121.

22 Ibid., 152.

23 Ibid., 147.

24 Ibid., 148.

25 Ibid., 138.

26 John Muir, *The Mountains of California* (Garden City, NY: Doubleday, 1961).

27 Martin Buber, *I and Thou*, trans. Ronald G. Smith (New York: Scribner, 1958).

28 John Muir, *The Writings of John Muir* (Boston: Houghton Mifflin, 1917–1918), "One Thousand Mile Walk," 301.

29 Herman Melville, *Moby-Dick or the White Whale* (New York: New American Library, 1961), 405.

30 Ibid., 196.

31 John Calvin, *Commentaries on the First Book of Moses Called Genesis*, trans. John King (Edinburgh: Edinburgh Printing, 1837), I, 106.

32 John Calvin, *Institutes of the Christian Religion*, trans. Ford Lewis Battles, ed. John T. McNeil (Philadelphia: Westminster, 1960), 1.14.20.

33 Calvin, *Genesis*, I, 57.

34 Muir, *Writings*, "Our National Parks," 328.

35 Muir, *Writings*, "Travels in Alaska," 84.

36 Richard Wrangham, *How Cooking Made Us Human* (New York: Basic Books, 2009).

37 Mark Molesky, *This Gulf of Fire: The Destruction of Lisbon, or Apocalypse in the Age of Science and Reason* (New York: Knopf, 2015). This book was reviewed by Matthew Price in the *Boston Globe*, November 4, 2015.

38 José Saramago, *Baltasar and Blimunda*, trans. Giovanni Pontiero (New York: Harcourt, 1982).

39 Fleming Rutledge, *The Crucifixion: Understanding the Death of Jesus Christ* (Grand Rapids: Eeerdmans, 2015).

40 "Beautiful Savior," *Evangelical Lutheran Worship* (Minneapolis: Augsburg Fortress, 2006), no. 838.

41 Joseph Sittler, "Called to Unity," in *Evocations of Grace*, 38–50.

42 For an assessment of Teilhard's significance in this context, see Santmire, *The Travail of Nature*, 155–74.

43 Moltmann, Jürgen, *God in Creation: A New Theology of Creation and the Spirit of God*, trans. Margaret Kohl (San Francisco: Harper & Row, 1984).

44 Elizabeth A. Johnson, *Ask the Beasts: Darwin and the God of Love* (New York: Bloomsbury, 2014).

45 Pope Francis, *Laudato Si'*.

Made in the USA
Middletown, DE
26 January 2018